TeenWise

Career Planning for Teens without College

Unlocking a World of Possibilities to Create a
Remarkable Future of Financial Security and
Meaningful Impact without a College Degree

By

Jonathan Reed

Table of contents

Introduction

Jan is a Ukrainian immigrant in California whose parents moved from Kyiv in his mid-teens. After arriving in California, Jan had to clean after customers at a local grocery so his family could stay financially afloat.

At 18, Jan realized he had a passion – a quiet enthusiasm about technology. Pursuing his newly-found interest, Jan borrowed manuals from a bookshop and taught himself computer networking.

Soon, Jan met a group of hacker friends who helped him improve his programming skills and linked him with brilliant minds and future tech gurus. Unknown to him, the passion he'd found and honed while scrambling for food stamps and government support alongside his family would make the bedrock for a legendary career.

Jan chose to boost his tech skills with a Math and Computer Science degree from San Jose State University. However, Jan would soon drop out of San Jose State.

The skills he'd already learned *proved* enough to convince David File, a Co-founder at Yahoo! to gift him a technical role at the IT company.

However, his brief time of study at San Jose wasn't a waste of time. While studying at college, Jan worked part-time at Ernst & Young, where he met Brian Acton, who'd later partner with him to create his breakthrough tech product – WhatsApp.

- End of the story - *at least for now.*

Why is Jan Koum's story the best for opening this teen finance masterpiece that teaches young people how to plan toward – and attain – career fulfillment and success?

It's a real-world illustration of how any teenager can chart a rewarding career for themselves – whether or not they choose to get a college degree.

Beyond that, Jan's story amplifies many precious gems I'll show you in this easy-to-read-AND-practice material.

This is NOT your regular teen motivation manual or finance hack book. It combines well-handpicked, tried, and tested weapons top industry professionals extol in practice.

TEENWISE: Career Planning without College for Teens is the perfect book for laying the foundation for financial security and a meaningful impact throughout your lifetime. And the best part?

You've already had enough education from high school to build a successful non-technical career! And even if you choose the technical route? *You already guessed right* – Jan's story and many others prove that you can become a highly successful tech entrepreneur without a degree.

Beyond learning how to chart a career path without a college degree, you'll learn how to maintain positive self-esteem, develop a can-do attitude, and hone your non-technical (or semi-technical) entrepreneurship prowess. Of course, I won't stop at that.

You'll also learn how to master financial literacy early and avoid grave mistakes many adults made that have seemingly marred their finances forever.

Now, this isn't to scare you – or discourage you from getting a college degree if you want. But the school system is failing youths and teenagers like you. It barely prepares you for the real world out there.

Introduction

Your teachers and professors would have you memorize random topics across various fields you may never need. Then add that to the boredom of a standardized test glass ceiling you must shatter to get to the next class – or avoid a retake.

Of course, I'm not against improving your memory or grades – and you should, at any school you attend.

However, a better way to prepare YOU for your desired future is building a curriculum that fosters:

✓ Critical thinking

✓ Problem-solving skills

✓ Intelligent financial management and

✓ Adaptability

These four aren't just cardinal to succeed in today's rapidly-evolving market. You'll need loads and loads of information on them – plus a sniper focus on each skill – to make them part of your everyday life.

And that leads me to the *just* one thing I need from you to maximize the invaluable tips in this book. It's the five-lettered word that separates the eagle from its contemporaries, among a few other qualities – F-O-C-U-S.

You've got to have, or develop, a focus on success, independence, confidence, happiness, and YOUR personal growth. You *need* to have enough determination and the desire to go all out to achieve your loftiest career goals.

Since success is best shared with others, I'll show you *how* to enjoy success – and reach out to less advantaged individuals or communities around you. That way, you can build a viable social capital for your brand, amplify your positive influence, and leave a lasting legacy for others coming behind. Oh, and you'll also find an engaging workbook at the end of each chapter, carefully written to help you reassess or apply the lessons of each chapter.

I'm sure you're itching to get into the book in full.

So am I.

Get ready for a memorable experience!

Part 1

Discovering Your Path

Now, back to Jan's story on how he moved from surviving on food stamps while working as a teenage cleaner so his newly migrant family could survive to become a billionaire after selling WhatsApp alongside co-founder Brian Acton.

It might seem needless to point this out, but Jan may have gone on to work for a Fortune 500 company like Ernst & Young and spent decades before becoming a Chief Technology Officer (if that ever happened) with his Math and Computer Science degree. Or even a college professor like his tutors at the Ivory Tower.

BUT – and a big *but* at that – chances are extremely small he'd have found as much satisfaction or fulfillment OR success in those career paths.

Do you want to know how successful business leaders and entrepreneurs like Jan Koum discovered their hidden passion and began pursuing their life's zest?

According to a Deloitte report, only 13% of America's workforce is passionate about their jobs. If anything, these stats show that finding a career path you'll love – is more difficult than it seems.

In this section, I'll take you on a walk into differentiating between societal/family expectations from your passion and unique path. You'll learn to appreciate unconventional career paths, often abundant with fun and the freedom to express your personality.

It'll take some days or weeks, in various ways, to apply the principles here and discover what career path genuinely and aptly fits your passion. But it's worth the read – I promise.

First, I stir your appetite with success stories of entrepreneurs who have unleashed their potential without (or before) college enough to lead successful careers for themselves and others in non-traditional career paths.

Then I show you how to set clear career goals, leverage apprenticeship and mentorship opportunities, and network with the Who's Who in your choice fields without a degree.

Of course, you affirm your readiness for a successful career while in your teens by building transferrable and relevant skills via various learning opportunities. I'll show you how to leverage remote work environments and other open-source educational platforms and maximize self-development.

It's about *you*. It's about *your career*. It's about planning a successful career while in your teens.

And I've got your back.

Let's dive in already! Yeah?!

Chapter 1

Unleashing Your Potential

Hide not your talents; they for use were made // What's a sundial in the shade?
– Benjamin Franklin

Debunking the Degree Myth

Identifying Your Passions and Interests

According to a survey by Indeed, three in five employers think their employees underperform because they lack passion for their work.

But that's not the catch.

A higher percentage (76%) of employers don't believe anyone can *learn* a passion.

There you have it. Going by Indeed's survey, chances are low you'll ever change your passions.

And yes, I agree with most respondents in Indeed's survey.

You want to identify what ticks you and makes you motivate yourself the most and tailor your career along those lines. Otherwise, you risk the opportunity to join the elite 20% of Americans who feel 'very passionate' about their jobs.

Of course, not the remaining 80% are dissatisfied with their careers. About 45% more people are 'satisfied' with their jobs.

But, dear teenager, the last thing you want is to settle for being average.

So, how do you choose a career path you'll both love and be passionate about?

Other chapters will discuss further crucial aspects of teen career planning for teens. But in this opening chapter, I share actionable tips to help you discover your interests and passions.

What Does a Passion Mean?

Let's take a cue from Merriam-Webster's dictionary. It defines passion as a 'strong liking or desire for or devotion to some activity, object, or concept.'

Note the words: 'desire,' 'strong liking,' and 'devotion.'

They'll color the trigger points we'll highlight soon to help you discover where your passion lies.

However, there's a catch here. Some young people confuse the term passion with their hobbies or 'interests.' Unfortunately, confusing these terms can influence you into making short-sighted career and financial decisions on your professional or entrepreneurial journey.

To better understand some young people's dilemma about these subjects, let's consider Rose, a hypothetical (something-I-made-up) character who picks up this book, *TEENWISE: Career Planning without College for Teens.*

17-year-old Rose passed her GCE papers after completing high school in the UK. She enjoys playing her favorite video games when exhausted from school and work. If she's not doing that, she's watching countless episodes of her favorite series, Bridgerton, to pass the time.

But Rose also loves her pets (and almost every other pet on the streets) and wants them to be safe and free from predators or poachers.

Then, all thanks to her Bridgerton heroines, Rose cares so much about her looks that she can't stand the slightest wrinkle on her face.

Rose wonders how to figure out her real passions among her most-loved activities. Perhaps becoming a Hollywood actress relieves the feeling of being *on set* and pretending before the camera. Maybe owning a video gaming franchise will make the best career fit.

Or what do you think?

She flips the coin from the entertainment sector to the animal sector and considers leading a social revolution to protect animals – or maybe owning an animal sanctuary later in life.

Lastly, she mentally leaves the world of pets and considers owning a spa or becoming a dermatologist.

However, Rose is reading this book and wonders where her passion or interests lie. Of course, she wants to build a rewarding career for herself.

Rose may be you. And she may be another tween around you finding it hard to prioritize among their hobbies and passions to plan their futures.

You see, there's actually no need to worry. It's going to be pretty easy to pinpoint your passions and set yourself on the path to finding an unconventional career or financial future.

Passions or Hobbies? Hmm. Trouble in Paradise.

I've shown that passion means a strong liking, desire, or devotion to something. It could be anything – an activity, object, or concept.

Conversely, a hobby is a pursuit outside of regular occupation, especially for relaxation. A helpful synonym for a hobby is 'recreation' – fun-time stuff.

While your passions motivate or inspire you to be productive, your hobbies may help you relax in between pursuing your passions or other interests.

This table helps to make the difference clearer.

Hobby	Passion
Something you pursue outside your regular occupation, often to relax	A strong desire for or devotion to something. It could be a concept, an activity, or an object.
Things you do for fun during your free time	It consumes most of your time. But you don't mind anyway.
Things you'll do to pass break times, holidays, and other free times	It runs in your veins like hemoglobin in the blood. You can't imagine life without it.
Doesn't necessarily fit into your core values or lofty ideals about how life should look or run	It often gains inspiration or motivation from your personal beliefs
You often don't desire to excel at it	You're more likely to seek excellence (at least improvements) in your skill
Think recreation acts like workout classes, video games, movies, shopping, or talking to friends	Think of socially impactful acts like leading a weekly sports club, an NGO, a mentoring platform, or doing research to save the planet.

So, between all four activities that Rose loves, which is/are most likely to be her passions or hobbies?

I hope you guessed correctly.

Rose would likely do great championing a cause that protects pets. She's also likely to perform excellently as a dermatologist.

However, although she loves the Bridgerton series, 17-year-old Rose would ditch her favorite acts for an Instagram live or community event that discusses animal safety.

Becoming a Hollywood/TV star isn't likely to make a great career for Rose. She'd also instantly stop using gamepads at the slightest discomfort she felt in her palms.

If you were Rose, becoming a skin-care professional (dermatologist, spa owner, cosmetologist – you name it) could be one of the best decisions you can make for yourself and humanity.

So, I guess you already understand why you need to choose a path for your financial and professional future around your passions – and not mere *fun*.

Once you understand how fundamental your passion and interests are, it's time to learn how to identify them.

Now, I just have to say this. Sometimes, that 'passion' may not be a money spinner. In that case, you need to find a money spinner somehow because, my friend, you can't enjoy your life enough to practice passion if you're not financially stable. More of this to come.

Find Your Passion Here – in 5 Easy Steps

1. What Are the Special Points in Your Day?

Look through your average day, and you'll find certain times in the day you look forward to. It could be anything from a specific meeting to an assigned task or a personal time you set aside.

Then, unexpected moments in your day could end up being the most memorable of the day/week. You want to notice every significant or seemingly insignificant detail around the peak moments in your day.

Some of these 'euphoric' moments might occur at work or school. Other high points include time-out with family, friends, or yourself. Look out for people and places that relate to these special moments; they'll prove helpful in helping you identify your passions – and, subsequently, your chosen career paths.

2. What Takes Your Money and Time?

Everyone, old and young, spends their resources on things they consider meaningful. How about reviewing your credit card statements, bank statements, and other records of your income/expenditure for recurring themes?

Then, move on to the topics of books, magazines, movies, or podcasts you spend time with. If possible, make an *actual* (not *mental*) list of their topics and look for recurring subjects.

Lastly, check out common themes between your passions and hobbies, especially those that have long stayed with you. Meanwhile, the interests you've held for the longest time may be more related to your passion than newly-picked hobbies.

3. What Topics Would You Love to Teach or Talk About?

Here's the place to consider your conversations with people around you. What interactions excite you the most? What's that topic you've found that always makes you *come alive* when it's under discussion?

It could also help to consider if there are any tasks or topics you'd love to teach others. Your passions are often not very far away.

4. What Are Your Skills?

I'll delve into identifying your strengths deeper shortly after this section in the chapter. But suffice it to say that your soft and hard skills can well point you toward your passions.

You know why?

You must have likely developed these hard or soft skills because they related to your passion in the first place. You want to look for natural skills that boost your confidence when faced with a task or assignment.

5. Review All the Details in 1-4 Together

Put together a detailed list of items, skills, people, and places you figured in points 1-4. Then review each piece of information to see how it fits an overall picture of your loftiest ideals and expectations in life.

So, suppose you find volunteering at a disabled people's home as the highest point in your day. You want to probe further by asking questions like, 'Why does spending time with disabled populations make me excited?'

It could be helping others, ensuring a healthier world, or even because of one patient in that home you love spending time with. Now, it doesn't have to be complicated.

It's your hobby, your interests, your desire, your passion. It's your life. And you've lived like that already.

See it as some exercise to probe yourself with some prying needles.

Deeply reviewing this information could take time, but it'll help you identify what motivates you and spur you on to seek a career related to your interests and passions, even if you don't pick up something perfectly describable as a hobby for you.

Understanding Your Unique Strengths and Skills

Remember I highlighted understanding your strengths and skills just some paragraphs earlier?

Billie Jean King, former world number 1 tennis player, once said, 'Self-awareness is probably the most important thing for becoming a champion.'

Understanding your unique strengths and skills can help you recognize environments (things, people, and places) that help you thrive and seek them.

And what if you already know your strengths?

Well, writing and analyzing them can help improve your ability to self-reflect and provide you with tips on how to deploy them.

Doing so can also help you periodically track your improvements toward recognizing new interests and track your improvements (and successes) throughout your career.

Are you ready to uncover your self-worth as a teen and grow genuine confidence to develop and present your brand to the world?

Get to know your strengths and identify them as accurately as you can.

First, What Are Your Strengths?

Your strengths include skills, attributes, and traits that can help you succeed. The combination of your strengths is often unique, sometimes resulting from your personality, education, or experiences.

Your strengths could include soft skills and traits that help you collaborate better with others. They could also include hard skills that make you technically competent in a field or area.

For instance, a combination of traits like high collaborative aptitude, analytical thinking skills, and logical reasoning with hard skills like programming languages and software design might be a great fit for an IT career.

How to Find Your Strengths as a Career-Wise Teen

1. Spot Your Passions (and Hobbies)

Everything we've discussed in the last section about identifying your passion or hobby will be useful here. Developing skills into key strengths around things you're passionate about is often easier.

For instance, tweens who enjoy painting during free time may be able to develop traits like patience, creativity, and attention to detail.

Meanwhile, while painting remains a hobby, they can apply the traits it develops into various careers like administrative duties, education, or architecture.

2. Feedbacks

One way to develop a more accurate self-awareness is by listening to what others say about you. However, your folks won't freely share their feedback unless they think you'd gladly welcome them.

Listen to what your coworkers, colleagues, dorm-mates, or roommates think about you and your performance at school. Try to recollect past times they gave positive feedback and check what actions elicited those compliments.

While maintaining open arms to feedback and reviews from people around you, intentionally request opinions from various people.

It could be your manager, a coworker, or even a mentee or student you tutor. People who relate with you can easily tell what specific aspects of your service or output benefit them the most.

Ask them to give concrete examples with helpful contexts that show how these suggestions might be your biggest strengths. Make a list of their recommendations and look out for common features to spot your most prominent strengths.

3. Take a Personality Test

There are tons of free and helpful personality tests out there that can help you recognize areas where you're already strong or successful. But they can also help you identify skill sets you're yet to experience.

Personality tests often evaluate interpersonal strengths like leadership qualities, emotional intelligence, and likely temperaments.

Attending to your personality test results will help you improve your relationship with others. Additionally, they'll help you learn how your strengths can complement others in the workplace and build a strong, professional network.

1. Explore New Experiences

Your self-awareness heavily depends on past experiences. One way to identify your strengths is by attempting new skills, hobbies, and activities.

Research opportunities to develop your career and skill sets regularly. Once in a while, step out by asking to collaborate on projects outside your routine tasks.

Opportunities to attend classes, learn new technical skills, shadow coworkers, or lead in new areas are excellent examples of new experiences you can explore. While trying something new, you may uncover novel strengths or other hidden skills and personality traits to guide your career plans.

70 Examples of Strengths You Might Possess

I've put up 70 examples of strengths you can discover in yourself as you apply the principles in this actionable section.

1.	Tenacity	5.	Sense of humor
2.	Logical aptitude	6.	Adaptability
3.	Leadership	7.	Critical thinking
4.	Confidence	8.	Risk-taking

9. Public speaking	30. Coding
10. Optimism	31. Training
11. Negotiation	32. Proactivity
12. Delegation	33. Diligence
13. Transparency	34. Email marketing
14. Discipline	35. Programming languages
15. Constructive criticism	36. Ambition
16. Empathy	37. Innovation
17. Patience	38. Forecasting
18. Writing	39. Emergency Preparedness
19. Enthusiasm	40. Risk management
20. Curiosity	41. Cultural competency
21. Honesty	42. Passion
22. Open-mindedness	43. Entrepreneurship
23. Performing	44. Positive attitude
24. Organization	45. Social skills
25. Coordination	46. Empowerment
26. Compassion	47. Charisma
27. Social media	48. Research
28. Community management	49. Multi-tasking
29. Compliance	50. Humility

51. Presentations

52. Client communication

53. Business strategy

54. Client communication

55. People management

56. Philanthropy

57. Machine learning

58. Time management

59. Experimentation

60. Decision making

61. Relationship-building

62. Loyalty

63. Tact

64. Active listening

65. Objectivity

66. Friendliness

67. Pop culture knowledge

68. Event planning

69. Work ethic

70. Emotional intelligence

Breaking Free from Societal Expectations

Now, one of the challenges young people face surrounds the struggle to break free from stereotypical expectations from people around them. You've probably had enough already.

If it's not your teacher 'pushing' you to make all A's, it's your mom or dad incessantly querying your desire to follow an unconventional career path.

Or it's the news blaring on all sides about the latest 'social values' Americans *should* have even though you can't personally relate to these *values*. It could be anyone, including your friends.

If you reside in America, you're already aware of the country's high and nearly unrealistic societal expectations. Worse still, attempting to break away from the status quo puts you at certain risks. For instance, you're likely to miss out on enjoyable, productive, or helpful relationships.

I perfectly understand where you are. I can relate – everyone around me had their expectations about what they thought I should do after college. And I must admit: it was sometimes intimidating.

However, you're best positioned to enjoy a fulfilling career when you practice self-awareness, identify your strengths, and gain confidence to share your passions with others.

Never Compromise You

Have you ever felt like a square peg trying to fit into a society that's as round as *round* can be? I bet!

In a world that often prioritizes conforming to preset molds, feeling like you don't belong is a common feeling for teens. Besides the weird feeling of being an alien in your immediate environment, young people tend to face a range of often harmful prejudices.

Ever suffered from racism, ageism, or elitism?

Sadly, we often fail to acknowledge that the world is beautifully diverse. Each person has unique strengths and qualities that may not blend into clear categories.

Now, here's a disclaimer. I've never been a fan of an aggressive and excessive *wokeness* that often confuses young people from being self-confident or secure in themselves.

 Instead, I'm advocating starting a journey to discover where you truly fit in today's world. That, my dear, is the best path to all the fulfillment and happiness you need.

And your lesson begins with this when you learn to never compromise your personality merely for the sake of fitting into society.

Everyone is unique and has some great things they can offer the world around them. Besides, being like someone else isn't a prerequisite.

You want to concentrate on friendships and connections that matter the most to you. Meanwhile, you also want to steer clear of folks who never see anything good enough in you to celebrate you.

While it can be challenging to assert yourself, it's less stressful than pretending to be who you are not.

Find Your Tribe

One interesting thing about finding a career path that suits your unique passions and interests is that you'll often find people like you – one way or another. Your immediate environment or friends might not find your passions intriguing enough. But there's always a 'tribe' that responds the same way as you do on some topics, careers, or educational paths.

Your tribe could be an online or offline group that emphasizes your values. They could also be mentors or role models whose values resonate with your budding interests. It can be amazing how much encouragement and friendship you can find in these relationships that make your tribe.

The Information Age advanced as fast as it has over the last three decades because frontliners in the industry sought a way out from the routine and boredom of the Industrial Age. Of course, each CEO, entrepreneur, or employee in the Information Age succeeded because they found people who supported their ideas (their tribe).

Suppose you're passionate about fashion; your tribe will likely include fashion enthusiasts like fashion designers, fashion bloggers, and fashion influencers.

You also want to note that your tribe mustn't include only (or any) people in your age range or around you. What you need most is a culturing environment for your passions to thrive.

Beyond humans, your tribe could also include new experiences or work environments that align with your passions. Finding your tribe can also involve developing a sense of purpose and meaning by volunteering with a not-for-profit or sharing your experiences with others.

In the end, the key to breaking free from societal expectations lies in embracing self-awareness and self-acceptance. Here's where to embrace your unique qualities and strengths and foster a sense of belonging independent of environmental approval or validation.

Next, we consider how embracing non-traditional career paths could help maximize your passions while fulfilling your financial and career dreams.

Exploring Non-Traditional Career Paths

In a post-COVID world, the idea of a conventional 9-5 job increasingly loses appeal to consumers and business owners globally. The need for flexibility, independence, and versatility have made many working-class individuals seek non-traditional career paths.

Interesting examples of non-traditional career paths include freelancing, entrepreneurship, remote work, creative arts, niche industries, and more.

A non-traditional career path involves a profession that challenges tradition or convention. The US Department of Labor defines a non-traditional career path as one in which 25% or less of those employed across the field are of a specific gender.

That means, besides the examples listed above, other examples of unconventional career paths would include:

- a male nurse

- a woman technician

- a lady firefighter

- a male flight attendant

- a female chef

- a male secretary/administrative assistant

I guess some of these roles sounded odd to your reading. It sure did to mine.

Well, if any didn't sound odd to you, you probably already understand this chapter: breaking stereotypes and rigid/baseless societal expectations.

As we saw in the last section, pursuing a non-linear career path would mean attempting to go against the grain of societal norms. And that would often come with challenges like discrimination, bias, stereotypes, and lack of support.

Why Non-Traditional Career Paths?

Caroline Castrillion, a Forbes Contributor, predicts that non-linear career paths are the future of work. To her, companies in recent times would employ *skilled* applicants without a degree or minimum years of experience.

By taking up a skills-based hiring approach rather than the 'paper-based' tradition, Castrillion suggests that companies can attract and retain top talents and cut the time or money involved in staffing.

Besides the risks involved in non-linear or self-taught career paths, what are the benefits of pursuing a non-traditional career path?

1.   More Opportunities to Express Your Passion and Creativity

Non-traditional career paths often originate from people with genuine talents and passion. And that becomes the measuring line for new employees or entrants in these industries.

Whether it's starting a socially-conscious business or becoming an artist, these non-traditional careers are great platforms to express your skills.

Besides being a faster route to earning your highest income, non-traditional career paths help you experience a sense of fulfillment that traditional careers may not provide.

2. Diverse Work Opportunities

Non-traditional career paths give you the liberty to explore diverse fields and industries. It allows you to adapt to changing market trends and take on exciting challenges while continuously improving your skill sets.

3. Professional and Personal Growth

Non-traditional career paths often facilitate work environments that encourage continuous learning. They'll require stepping outside their comfort zone to embrace novel challenges.

Additionally, the non-linear professional is often exposed to new ideas, industries, and approaches to overcome unconventional challenges or conventional challenges unconventionally.

Once you find a suitable non-traditional role, you'll be amazed at the impacts of personal and career developments on your profile. They are often rewarding, grit-building, and resilience-fostering in various ways.

Freelancer. Entrepreneur. Remote Worker.

Going by the US DoL's definition, many other unconventional career paths exist.

But let's sneak peek into three popular non-traditional career paths: remote work, freelancing, and entrepreneurship.

Remote work allows you to work from anywhere globally once you can connect to the internet. One of the most flexible unconventional career paths, remote workers can function in various fields.

Popular remote work fields include customer service, programming, graphic design, and writing.

Entrepreneurs start their businesses, taking full responsibility for their successes or failures. Besides the high level of independence and control entrepreneurship affords founders, it pressures them to build and develop themselves.

While startup founders can work in any industry, they typically concentrate on creating innovative services and products that meet a need in the market.

Freelancers work on a project-by-project basis, often juggling various contracts for multiple clients at once. Freelancing lets you choose who you want to work with, what projects you want to work on, and when you're ready to exit or fly to your favorite destination on vacation.

Freelancers, remote workers, and entrepreneurs share common ground. Freelancers, like remote workers, could work in various fields like tech, marketing, copywriting, administrative assistance, and more.

Remote work offers the freedom to work from anywhere. Although remote work can require a large degree of self-discipline and can be isolating, the prospects of developing healthy emotional habits and work ethics are immense.

Similarly, freelancing gives you a high rate of freedom and control over your work. However, it requires self-discipline and self-motivation to thrive in this path.

While the high-earning potentials of entrepreneurship are high, it require significant investment of resources and an understanding of business dynamics.

But there's no need to worry about developing the necessary skills for a successful non-linear career. The success stories you'll find in the next subsection and other career development tips will inspire and show you how.

It's time to begin charting a successful career path for yourself as a teen.

Success Stories

Success doesn't always come easy. More often than not, it's a fruit of tireless/continuous labor. You only need to ask other budding entrepreneurs, leaders, and influencers around you to see how true that is.

Many would tell you of challenging, persistent, and tiresome processes that kept them awake several nights and made them miss plenty of playing or recreational time.

However, as you keep up in your pursuit of career success, learning about the stories of successful entrepreneurs, industry leaders, and social change agents can boost your morale and gear you up.

You can take it from me. Going on a non-traditional career path or starting a business from scratch would be one of the most frightening tasks in the world.

However, you don't want to focus your energy on how things could fail or how you could end up 40% into your plans. Concentrate on how things could go right, and your name could join a similar list like the one in this section.

Meanwhile, if you go through many success stories, you'll find that many of your role models failed sometime in their lives. But they didn't let their failures and struggles prevent them from reaching for gold.

Today, figuring out how you can get your ideas off the ground might look challenging and nearly insurmountable. However, with the technological advancements of 2023, you couldn't have it easier developing your brand or proposal and getting it in front of the right people.

MaryBeth Hyland – Founder, Spark Vision

MaryBeth's story is one of the most inspiring entrepreneurial stories. After surviving lots of abuse in her early life, MaryBeth battled low self-esteem.

However, she disregarded her struggles and diverted her energy into creating Spark Vision. Spark Vision helps businesses collaborate with teams from other organizations, facilitating a collaborative office workspace rid of toxicity.

Her ability to gain freedom from an abusive childhood and debilitating work experiences has helped her excel in engaging millennials. With her husband, James, MaryBeth holds regular sessions with professionals, teaching them mindfulness via MaryBeth & James Hyland.

Hyland refused to let others take life from her and converted her pain and hurt into creating an amazing business that facilitates a healthy office culture. Her model isn't only financially successful; it also impacts others to become better.

Itamar Gero, SEOreseller

Itamar began showing interest in entrepreneurship and programming when he was young. That probably spurred him to sell his first commercial software at 16, and he went on to create many other successful companies like Axadra Ventures, Siteoscope.com, and SkillFuel.com.

Later, Itamar Gero went on to serve in the Israeli army as an IT specialist. In 2011, 32-year-old Itamar founded SEOReseller.com, a white-label digital marketing firm. He leveraged his years of experience in software development, SaaS building, marketing, and search engine optimization (SEO) to build SEOReseller.

The digital marketing firm introduced novel service delivery and creativity to an industry heavily dependent on outdated techniques like Excel sheets and emails. Today, his remarkable commercial aptitude has earned him a role as President of the Israel Chamber of Commerce, fostering business relationships between Israel and the Philippines.

Sophia Amoruso

Sophia is an inspiration to many female entrepreneurs and fashionistas.

26

Young Sophia was diagnosed with ADHD, which prevented her from coping at school.

Consequently, she had to leave school. She soon had to run odd jobs, including waiting at restaurants like Subway. But things got even worse for Amoruso after her parents' divorce forced her to relocate to Sacramento, California.

During this period, poverty forced her to survive by shoplifting, hitchhiking, and stealing from dustbins.

But a turnaround came for Amoruso in 2006, when she got fed up with her situation. She began fighting her way to a successful career and lifestyle. That resolve led her to find Nasty Gal Vintage on eBay.

Nasty Gal Vintage kicked off as Amoruso searched the racks at second-hand stores and sold them online. She converted proceeds from her sale to purchase a walk-in warehouse that attracted customers from various social media platforms.

While her business grew slowly initially, she kept pushing the limits. By 2008, she recorded revenue of $223,000. Only three years later, her income stood at $23 million, earning her the appellation 'The Cinderella of Tech' on the cover of a New York Times production.

While Amoruso recently lost about half her wealth, which peaked at $280 million in 2016, she's still a rising star. Her story shows that life is full of ups and downs, *and* ups and downs. A humble background might be one of the greatest struggles for a young person. But it doesn't stop them from creating an inspiring story of successful entrepreneurship.

Richard Branson

Richard Branson is a name you couldn't easily omit when coming up with a list of successful entrepreneurs and their stories. Richard Branson switched from business to business for 40 years, seemingly interested in testing his business acumen against virtually everything.

Richard was diagnosed with dyslexia, a learning disorder characterized by difficulty in reading, at a young age. This made him a poor student who often struggled with his subjects.

It's also probably why he earned the title 'Virgin' when he started his first business at a very young age. He was *a virgin* at entrepreneurship, and for his age, folks around him felt he deserved the adjective as a proper noun.

However, Branson turned all the mocking and laughing into a household name for himself with his first business. By the 1960s, he began importing and re-selling music records while he began managing the Student magazine.

His hard work spurred him to open a London record store in 1971. Like many other successful entrepreneurs, Branson reinvested money he got from selling other people's products into building his company, Virgin Records.

He built his record label by leveraging relationships like the Rolling Stones he made while he corresponded for the Student. Beyond 1971, Branson developed several products and services that became popular worldwide, including Virgin Airlines.

As of 2023, Branson is worth approximately $3 billion and hasn't stopped investing in various businesses and companies. Branson's story summarizes some of his life lessons in this quote to future billionaires:

'Don't wait to start until you have all your investment in place … in many cases, you don't need lots of money to start a business.'

Oprah Winfrey

Golden Globe winner and global icon Oprah Winfrey wasn't born as the powerful woman you know her to be today. Born into a poor home in rural Mississippi, Oprah looked far from what her future would turn out to be.

After surviving a troubled childhood, Oprah got a role in a radio station while in high school. By 19, she became a co-anchor for the local evening news and later a daytime talk-show host.

After years of gaining experience working for others, Oprah Winfrey began her own production company. Hitting her first million dollars at age 32, Oprah would not stop growing her wealth. She eventually amassed a net worth of $800 million and earned the recognition of being the richest African American of the 20th Century.

Today, with a Forbes-estimated net worth of $2.5 billion, Oprah is one of the wealthiest self-made women in the United States of America. If Oprah were to give teens one tip on spending money, it would be this: 'Spend/invest your money only on/in things you truly believe in.'

Workbook 1

Make a list of things you love to do or talk about, categorizing them into hobbies and passions based on what you've learned in this chapter.

Take a specialized personality test for teenagers. What do you think about the results? Share your observations on the results with a trusted friend or mentor.

Takeaway 1

There are beautiful lessons all through this chapter. However, if there is one thing I want you to leave with as you join me in the next chapter, it'll be a snippet from Sophia Amoruso's story.

"Life is full of ups and downs, *and* ups and downs … But it doesn't stop YOU from creating an inspiring story of successful leadership, entrepreneurship, and positive influence.

Chapter 2

Crafting Your Career Path

Luck is what happens when preparation meets opportunity
- Seneca

Setting clear career goals

Self-assessment

Self-assessment allows you to evaluate yourself and allows you to improve your decision-making process or make more informed choices.

As you study, work, and relate with others, you're already subconsciously evaluating yourself. However, self-assessment is a rather conscious way to evaluate your growth, preferences, talents, opportunities, and threats to set clear career goals.

Fortunately, self-assessment goes beyond planning your professional career. You can fit self-assessments into other aspects of your life, work, or studies to help determine what set of goals you should pursue next.

Why Must I Conduct Self-Assessment?

Self-assessment involves knowing more about yourself and measuring your growth. You may also perform these tests based on various criteria, ranging from emotional intelligence to hard skills or mental aptitude.

Here are some reasons to assess yourself before planning a career or financial plan that fits. A thorough self-assessment helps you:

✓ Understand your strengths and weaknesses

✓ Better understand how well you perform at a role

✓ Create attainable and ambitious goals

✓ Become motivated to develop

4 Actionable Steps to Conducting a Thorough Self-Assessment

1. Highlight Your Proudest Moments

Yes, this might not be what you'd expect in my 4-step guide to conducting a thorough self-assessment. But you couldn't truly evaluate yourself if you disregarded milestones in your experience.

Highlight your proudest moments, remembering significant milestones in your educational and professional development. A great way to do this is to highlight specific tasks, projects, or assignments that best showcase your abilities.

While pointing out the events or tasks that led to your feats, highlight your success's impact on yourself, your family, your business, your team, or your school. That way, you'd encourage yourself to repeat those feats in future occupations and roles.

2. Sincerely Critique Your Experiences

Of course, self-assessments go beyond highlighting your successes. They also involve critiquing downtimes to come away with an important lesson. By identifying your flaws, shortcomings, excesses, and failures, you can better demonstrate the ability to learn and develop.

Meanwhile, you don't want to be self-deprecating during your assessment.

As a top executive at Harvard Business School puts it, it'd help to use 'developmental language' when critiquing areas that need improvement.

For instance, 'I suck at meeting deadlines,' why not say, 'I want to work on my punctuality. Here's what I've learned. Here's what I should do afterward.' Maintaining an overall positive mindset when critiquing yourself can help you maintain a healthy self-esteem and spur you toward your goal rather than discourage your efforts.

3. Keep Striving for Growth

Humans are always growing and learning new things (whether or not they want to). However, it's not clear whether they're being productive with their growth or additional knowledge.

Regardless of your previous performances, staying committed to improving and educating yourself during self-critiquing sessions is vital. Here's the time to set reviewed goals and objectives for the next season or year.

That's how to indicate that you aren't settling for less.

Suppose you discovered areas needing improvement, such as your relationship with younger or less-experienced teens. You showcase your willingness to grow by setting clear targets to become a better leader/senior/influencer.

Conversely, suppose you identify areas where you perform excellently, like faithfully saving an amount or maintaining your New Year resolution on monthly workout classes. You'll do great to develop novel resolutions and saving targets toward the New Year to avoid boredom and stagnation.

4. Track Your Progress

Tracking your progress could include providing stats that reflect your accomplishments throughout a review period. Here's the place to supply concrete numbers to define your evaluated progress rate.

Doing this doesn't have to be complex or require complex analytics tools or software. Consider taking as little as 30 seconds daily to write your biggest achievement or success rate in a journal.

That can save you lots of memory stress during review time and give little room for guesswork on your efforts' effectiveness.

You don't want to handle any of these four steps lightly. Treat your self-assessment like a delicate work of art that pieces together in time. It'll shorten the time to achieve your set career and financial goals.

Goal setting

The Cambridge Dictionary defines goal setting as 'the process of deciding what you want to achieve or what you want someone else to achieve over a particular period ...'

And that's what it looks like.

However, I prefer Brian Tracy's definition of the same topic. The Canadian-American motivational public speaker and author says goal setting is 'the process of living with intention and letting life happen FOR us rather than TO us.'

I saw a metaphor used by James Clear, speaker and author of *Atomic Habits*, that aptly explains the idea of goal setting.

Oars and Rudders

James Clear wants us to imagine a small row boat. Our goals are the rudder on the boat, setting the direction for our movements.

When we commit to one goal, the rudder stays in place and keeps moving us forward. However, if we flip among goals, the rudder moves all around, making it easy to find ourselves rowing in circles.

Lastly, James Clear identifies another part of the boat he says is more important than the rudder: the oars. While the rudder signifies our goals, the oars are *how* we achieve them. The rudder determines our direction, but the oars decide how far we progress.

With this metaphor, James Clear helps to distinguish between systems and goals (oars and rudder).

So, suppose your goal is to save enough in the first quarter of next year to invest in a crowdfunding platform. Your system would be your monthly savings schedule.

Why Is Goal Setting Important?

When you meet your set goals, you'll gain more satisfaction and success than you would otherwise. However, the goal-setting process itself has many advantages that make setting goals crucial.

Just like the boat's rudder in James Clear's metaphor, setting goals helps you focus in a direction. Beyond that, predefined goals give you the chance to measure your progress. By keeping track of your current performance, you can reward productive efforts and identify areas that need improvement.

Moreover, goal-setting helps you avoid procrastination or keep time wastage to the barest minimum. Lastly, goals push you toward the next rung of the ladder and your chosen career or profession. Striving to meet and surpass goals can motivate you to achieve more than you'd have thought possible.

Setting Achievable Goals

1. Write Your Goals

You increase your chances of reaching your goals when you write them down by 33%, according to a study by Australian Psychologist Gail Matthews. Matthews also found in the same study that over 70% of respondents successfully met their goals when they sent weekly updates to others.

Another study by Nuclear Engineer and neuroscientist Mark Murphy showed that people who vividly describe their goals are 1.2 to 1.4 times more likely to meet them.

Write your goals regularly or somewhere you can see them. Read them aloud to yourself when you wake up and before you sleep. Keep them on top of your mind, and you have already increased your chances of meeting (or surpassing) them.

2. Keep Them Simple

Continuous changes are better than sudden demands to improve. It helps to concentrate your resources and mental energy on one or two goals at once.

Avoid coming up with a list of 'Ten career and lifestyle goals to achieve in the next ten months.' That could lead you into a mental challenge psychologists call 'goal competition' or 'goal conflict,' when two goals prevent each other.

3. Create SMART Goals

Edwin Locke and Gary Latham developed the concept of SMART Goals in their book, *A Theory of Goal Setting & Task Performance.*

According to them, SMART's Goals are:

- Specific

- Measurable

- Achievable

- Relevant; and

- Time-bound

You want to set specific goals relevant to your overall life's passion and values. Create a metric that helps you know how far you've progressed over a definite timeline.

Lastly, avoid setting goals you lack the skills and resources to realize. Set attainable goals and challenge yourself to attain them within your preset timelines.

However, what if you don't eventually meet your goals? Then this quote from Bruce Lee should come in handy,

'A goal is not always meant to be reached; it often serves simply as something to aim at.'

You'd have made significant progress in your personal development than you would without pursuing SMART goals.

4. Align Your Environment with Your Goals

Remove distractions, organize your environment, and relate often with positive-minded people who motivate you to achieve your goals.

Distractions can include anything from placing your phone in another room during work hours to removing junk food from your drawers when you're building a healthy weight.

Organize and plan around the systems you create to pursue your goals. So, suppose you need to read 30 minutes of a helpful guide at night. Preparing could mean getting some noise-canceling headphones to keep exterior noise away. It could also demand setting four alarms between 2 hours before the scheduled time so you don't forget.

Lastly, involve positive people and systems that encourage you to pursue your goals. Here's the place to identify helpful friends, role models, inspirational books, and music that can help keep you focused on the success you want to achieve.

Researching High-Demand Industries and Occupations

Many employers hire competent hands to bring on board without demanding a degree. Researching high-demand opportunities and industries can be helpful before deciding the best career path for you.

LinkedIn Most In-Demand Jobs (Q2, 2022)

Check out LinkedIn's most demanded jobs in the second quarter of 2022. This isn't exhaustive, but it provides an overview of highly sought-after roles.

1. Software engineer

2. Registered Nurse

3. Javascript Developer

4. Salesperson

5. Java Software Engineer

6. Project Manager

7. Delivery Driver

8. DevOps Engineer

9. Full Stack Engineer

10. Customer Service Representative

Meanwhile, the fastest growing roles in the same quarter on LinkedIn are:

1. Training Supervisor

2. Patient Service Representative

3. Physical Therapist

4. Distribution Specialist

5. Delivery Driver

6. Office Coordinator

7. Pediatric Nurse

8. Kitchen Staff

9. Oracle Specialist

10. Brand Representative

A report from Nasdaq partly agrees with LinkedIn's findings, observing that tech skills are the most in-demand skills in the U.S. Finally, let's see one more point of reference on what's going on in today's job market, the U.S. Bureau of Labor Statistics (BLS).

According to the BLS, these roles will see the highest projected percent employment change between 2020 and 2030.

1. Motion picture projectionists

2. Wind turbine service technicians

3. Ushers, lobby attendants, and ticket takers

4. Nurse practitioners

5. Solar photovoltaic installers

6. Restaurant cooks

7. Agents and business managers of artists, performers, and athletes

8. Customer attendants

9. Exercise trainers and group fitness instructors

10. Wooden model makers

By this stage, you've already identified your passions, interests, and financial or career goals. Having these narrows your search beam against shiny job alternatives that often distract many in their search for a profitable job or career path.

In addition, you might want to filter between the following options before setting out to pursue high-demand industries and occupations:

- Startup vs. established company?

- Work from home vs. Office desk?

- Is there any industry in mind already?

- What salary range am I looking at? (Be realistic to define a range that covers your needs.)

- Do I need a better salary, career growth, and autonomy? Which of these can I sacrifice?

The answers to these questions will help you decide the best positions to pursue and prepare you to follow them.

Even at this stage, you don't want to put all your eggs into one basket. Before sending any resumes, look for vacancies and companies matching your criteria. Filter through job boards, Linkedin, your network, college alumni, family, and friends for opportunities.

You can research LinkedIn jobs or roles by:

- Using the job-search function for words like 'tech recruiter' or 'hiring customer service representative.'

- Searching for hashtags related to your roles or preferred industries

- Leveraging advantage of your professional network

America's Big Tech companies will always indicate when there are open positions. (Meanwhile, the big tech companies are also called FAANG, and they include– Meta (formerly Facebook), Amazon, Apple, Netflix, and Alphabet (formerly Google)). Even when a division isn't hiring, they may gather applications for a hiring season.

If working with medium-sized organizations appeals to you, consider networking around titles in your preferred teams to locate the jobs.

Look out for vacancies in government and city forums regardless of your preferred industry or occupation. That's because governmental institutions need everything from cybersecurity to financial admins, truck drivers, and teachers.

Remember to properly research the job description of every ad, the company, and the team. Verify if you'd be glad to work with that organization. Lastly, keep a detailed record of every ad, brand, or opportunity that matches your criteria.

Not sure where to start searching for in-demand industries or opportunities? Start with a Google Search for 'Top Companies for (your target position, skill, or passion)' or 'Best Employers in (your preferred industry)'.

Generally, you couldn't go wrong choosing a career in tech, nursing, finance, human resources, or education.

Mind you, *in-demand* doesn't necessarily mean high-paying. It, however, suggests areas where the most movements are. For instance, bakers and other restaurant workers are in high demand partly because their workers seek more pay elsewhere. However, it's still important to know about industries and occupations less likely to lay off staff or get into a recession.

Create a list of companies with openings that match your profile. LinkedIn groups and job boards are also great. You may also want to create a list of 15 to 20 companies.

Don't be scared of trying many opportunities so you don't run out of alternatives later. Also, be ready to accept several rejections on your applications. It's an important part of preparing to find excellent opportunities.

Finding the right job will always require some preparation, vigilance, grit, and a willingness to adapt. However, in the end, persistence in sourcing the right information and taking informed steps will pay off.

Building a Personalized Career Roadmap

Here, we take a step further from just setting goals to creating a solid roadmap with the necessary milestones that create a clear path toward a successful career.

Leaders and entrepreneurs often use career roadmaps to advance their skills and achievements, whether remote workers, freelancers, employees, or boardroom staff.

After clarifying what I mean by a career roadmap and why it's vital for you, I'll show you how to create an efficient plan for your career and financial goals.

What Is a Career Roadmap, and Why Create One?

A career roadmap visualizes the steps you need to take toward reaching your professional goal. Your intended destination could be

- ✓ a high-ranking position in a company

- ✓ Multiplying your annual earnings

- ✓ a better job role

- ✓ attaining a well-defined status as an influencer or leader in a niche

An effective career roadmap includes:

- Where you are now

- What you want to achieve in your career

- An overview of the obstacles and skill gaps you must overcome to reach the destination

- The plan to overcome the obstacles and skill gaps to arrive at your destination

Identifying skill gaps can help you create an effective plan to acquire or boost these skills through various resources like:

- Books

- Workshops

- 1-1 Sessions

- Online courses

- Mentorships

A personalized career roadmap is a guiding map that helps you navigate your professional path with intentionality and purpose. Instead of adapting to opportunities your career *brings*, you want to *make* these opportunities happen because you know they'll help you get to your eventual destination.

Mapping out Crucial Milestones

You've established your current situation, goals, and the necessary obstacles to overcome. Next, break down your long-term goals into smaller, achievable steps (or milestones). These milestones will serve as progress indicators as you move from where you are to where you want to be in your career.

An Example of a Detailed Career Roadmap

Long-Term Goal

Launch a not-for-profit organization that includes at least 5 team members within the next two years.

Shorter-Term Goals

A. Gain knowledge on Leading NGOs and Social Causes (3-4 Months).

- Enroll in a course that teaches the methods, principles, and tools for running an NGO or championing a social cause.

- Attend seminars, workshops, webinars, or meets to learn industry best practices and trends in NGO leadership and management.

B. Apply NGO Management Skills in Current Role (4-6 Months)

- Identify opportunities in your current role or team that allow you to lead social causes, such as caring for other team members or recommending a CSR project to your circle.

- Seek overt and covert feedback from your friends, colleagues, or superiors on your management or leadership skills and demonstrate competence.

C. Seek Project Management Certification (6-12 Months).

- Research and obtain a certification in NGO leadership, management, and running.

- Prepare for the examinations by attending courses and studying relevant materials.

- Complete the certification exam to validate your project management skills and boost your credibility to lead an NGO or champion a cause.

D. Seek NGO Volunteering Opportunities Via Networking (12-18 Months)

- Attend conferences, networking sessions, and conferences to link with NGO professionals and leaders and expand your professional network.

- Seek volunteering opportunities to lead or join a CSR team in your current organization or explore vacancies in other teams.

E. Leverage Existing and New Networks toward Launching Your Team.

- Speak with friends, family, mentors, and role models about your team's vision.

- Seek collaborations that may include friends, peers, colleagues, and possibly an advisory member to create your team.

- Outline your brand's goals clearly, apply all lessons learned in the last 18 months and prepare to launch your brand.

Leveraging Apprenticeships, Mentorships, Vocational Training, and Certification Programs

Mentorship, vocational training, apprenticeships, and certification programs help you gain wisdom and skill from people with the experience, connections, and knowledge you crave. They play a crucial role in skill development, with many benefits for teens.

Whether it's beginning a mentorship journey, an apprenticeship program, vocational training, or a certification program, successful followership has pretty much the same principles.

Here's how to maximize your mentor's network and expertise, leverage their resources, and gain insights for your benefit.

Key Elements of an Effective Mentorship, Vocational, Apprenticeship or Certification Program

Here are five key elements to concentrate on to make your mentorship, vocational, apprenticeship, or certification program effective.

1. Select the Right Mentors or Programs

The success of your followership journey depends on selecting the right mentors. Here's the time to identify individuals, leaders, and professionals with the necessary skills, experience, and passion to teach and guide others.

Remember, the right mentors shouldn't just be experts in their fields. Choose professionals who also show strong interpersonal and communication skills.

2. Establish Clear Goals and Expectations from the Program

Why are you networking with this mentor? Why are you taking up the vocational program or certification program?

Define specific learning objectives and communicate them effectively to your mentors, tutors, and leaders. Remember to share information on how you can contribute to the connection.

Doing so will help you track your progress occasionally, evaluate the mentorship's effectiveness, and remain focused on your overall career goals. For instance, if learning project management best practices are your bottom line, make it clear to your mentor so that you learn as much as you can, and possibly share how you intend to reward their contributions directly or indirectly.

3. Create Trust and Rapport with Your Mentors/Tutors

Creating a strong relationship with your mentors or tutors is vital to tapping into their network and expertise. Trust and rapport are important for any mentorship or apprenticeship program to succeed. They create room for open and two-way communication, feedback, and sharing of challenges and successes.

You also want to be respectful and punctual. Prepare for every contact with your mentor or tutor. Demonstrate genuine interest for every time or advice they share with you. Show appreciation for their contribution from time to time.

Meanwhile, stay honest about your strengths and weaknesses while learning to adopt or understand your mentor or tutor's perspective and goals.

4. Request Further Introductions and Referrals

One of the leading benefits of having a mentor is that they can introduce you to other mentors or leaders who can help you advance your career. Your trainer's network may also include potential clients, employers, influencers, or collaborators in your niche. Say a thank-you whenever they make you a referral or introduce you to a position and update the outcomes.

5. Seek Feedback and Guidance

Feedback and guidance from a mentor, tutor, or trainer are invaluable in building your career. Your mentor's expertise can help you grow your performance, recognize opportunities, and overcome challenges.

Be open to constructive criticism and suggestions, asking relevant questions while also paying attention to their insights and perspectives. Appreciate their input and share your successes, failures, or other feedback with them.

How to Use LinkedIn to Find Apprenticeship, Mentorships, Vocational Training, and Certification Opportunities

✓ Search for a keyword on a job, position, or job you're interested in.

✓ Locate the companies, people, or posts that come with the search results.

✓ From the company page, go to 'People'. (At this stage, you have people in companies you intend to work for or who posted information you're interested in.)

✓ Study the 'People' you've found and determine if you have any 'connections in common with any of them.

✓ If yes, see who that 'connection' is (usually someone in your network), and send them a direct message.

✓ You could send the person a direct message like:

✓ 'Hi (Name), I saw you're connected to (So-and-so who works at this company) on LinkedIn. I just discovered a role I'm interested in and would love to connect to (Name) to introduce myself to them. Are you close enough to this person to either connect me with them or introduce us with this in mind? Thank you!'

✓ Once you get connected to them, send an elevator pitch introducing yourself and your intentions.

✓ Apply to the opportunity via the internal referral or direct connection, and you're ready to locate your remote job.

Pursuing Remote Work Opportunities

Remote work has been disrupting traditional workplace norms over the last decade and has gained significant popularity recently. Thanks to technological advancements and increasing globalization, a teen from Alaska can work remotely with other professionals on the other end of the globe.

I consider the remote work system an excellent one everyone should have some taste in. Besides the flexibility with working hours they afford workers, remote work helps companies access many more workers than they would otherwise. Mind you, remote work can be a lifesaver during moments of recession or financial difficulty, allowing many people to stay afloat.

Follow these steps to get a remote job within the next twelve months, or even 30 days – with no experience working remotely. Next, I've hand-picked some of the best remote jobs to pursue in 2023.

1. Decide If Working Remotely is for You

If you're considering a remote job, consider whether being physically away from family and colleagues is okay. Do you prefer personal interaction over alone time? Do you get motivated by working with your colleagues in a room?

Do the perks of an office, like in-person briefings, PCs, and desks, appeal to you? Even though you can work around these features in a remote work setting, it's less pronounced when working from home.

However, remember that remote jobs come with their benefits. For instance, high-paying remote work can help you save toward your big dreams. They also help you save money you'd have spent commuting or getting ready for work.

However, while considering your options, stay positive and adaptable to the varying situations. Remember to juggle between your interests, challenges, wants, and needs.

Knowing these can help you discover what inconveniences you can accommodate and which ones you can't overlook.

2. Get Ready for Your Remote Job Application Package

Get the following ready before beginning your remote job application:

- A stand-out resume or CV detailing your achievements, certifications, and experiences. Remember to tailor your CV to the role while putting as many valuable experiences as possible. (Without being verbose, feel free to extend your CV beyond the first page.)

- A few professional references with their names, emails, and phone numbers presentable during any interviews.

- A few excellent go-to responses for open-ended questions on application forms or interviews.

If you have no experience working remotely, it could help to pick up a remote side hustle or volunteer in a part-time remote role. What if you still couldn't find a remote part-time role?

In fields or niches where you can create a portfolio at home, e.g., in skills like graphic design, copywriting, or web design, take some time to create a portfolio you can present to potential employers and demonstrate your competence or expertise.

Suppose you're considering niches or industries where creating a portfolio from home might not be practical enough, e.g., administrative assistant, customer service representative, etc. Think about times you worked at home for any reason or adapt skills you've gained when handling other responsibilities that can contribute to the new team's goals or expectations.

3. Search for Remote Working Opportunities

Here, you'll need everything I said in the penultimate section on leveraging apprenticeships, mentorships, vocational training, and certification programs. In addition to LinkedIn job searches, search online by keywords for remote job listings on sites like Flexjobs, JustRemote, Indeed, Remote Woman, and more.

4. Ace the Remote Interview Process

A remote job role will most likely require a virtual interview via video or email correspondence. Consider getting prepared answers to some questions you might receive during the interview. Ask your mentors or other people already working in these organizations for tips on preparing and acing the interview!

Once the interview is over, send a thank-you note to the recruiters who interviewed you for the role you applied for while reminding them of your interest.

5. Follow Up Respectfully If You Don't Get a Feedback

Suppose you don't hear from your recruiter in two weeks. It'd help to send a follow-up letter. Remind them of your interest in the role, asking for any updates regarding the hiring process for this opportunity.

6. Accept Your Remote Job Offer or ...

Congratulations if you got the role! Remember to negotiate your offer and ensure it's a great fit for you before accepting it. You can now work from almost anywhere and travel worldwide at your pace or schedule.

And if you failed to get the role? Congratulations still – pat yourself on the back for attempting to advance your career. Another important life skill you'd learn is learning to cope with, overcome rejections, and stay focused. Review your application to see what improvements are necessary subsequently and concentrate on other applications.

Utilizing Online Resources and Platforms for Skill Development

Online learning is an excellent way to advance your career and meet your professional goals. However, how do you maximize these opportunities in creating a career development plan that fits your goals and passions?

Here are tips and strategies to help.

1. Identify and Clarify Your Learning Needs and Goals

What skills, knowledge, or credentials do you want to gain or improve? How do your learning needs and goals align with your interests and career aspirations? How will they benefit you in your current or future roles?

Once you identify what you want to learn and why, search for online courses, programs, or certifications that match your budget, time, and criteria.

2. Choose Quality and Relevant Online Courses

Next, choose only quality and relevant online courses. There are many options out there offering various paid or free learning opportunities. While some are instructor-led, others are self-paced.

Avoid identifying too many companies to follow to avoid overpaying or over-registering for you. Start with one; stick with it for a few weeks. If necessary, switch to better online course platforms or additional skills for a better learning experience.

3. Participate in Digital Learning Communities

Online learning communities contain learners who collaborate, interact, and support one another via online platforms like forums, social media, and chat groups. Participating in these digital learning communities can boost your learning experience and grow your professional network.

Ask relevant questions, share resources to help other learners, and receive feedback on your work. If you can't find an online learning community that fits your course or topic, consider creating your own with peers or mentors.

4. Follow Up and Maintain Online Networking Relationships

Your digital learning experience must have connected you to helpful professional networks and learning communities. Follow up on these relationships by building trust, rapport, and value with each connection.

Regularly provide feedback, share information, or offer help to people in your network. Celebrate others' milestones and achievements while also expressing gratitude to those who care about your progress.

Lastly, don't forget to track your learning and networking activities against your learning goals. Measure your results and adjust your strategies to emphasize more effective actions. Where some platforms don't fit your goals, consider switching to another platform or refocusing your efforts on other activities.

3 of My Favorite Online Platforms to Develop Your Skills

There are many digital learning platforms to develop your skills and advance your career. However, I've highlighted 3 of my favorite learning platforms here. Whether you're a teen learner, leader, or influencer, you can leverage these platforms to boost your entrepreneurial and leadership skills and prepare for a great career.

- **Coursera**

Coursera includes courses from leading experts and instructors from the best universities in the world. Teens interested in training and continuous learning can access video lectures, community discussion forums, and auto-graded or peer-reviewed assignments.

Coursera contains both free and paid content, as well as university-recognized degrees. You'd have the chance to choose from hundreds of courses and several tracks ranging from software training to business skills and Google Cloud certifications.

- **LinkedIn Learning**

LinkedIn Learning is an online video training library offering hundreds of courses on basic business topics. This platform lets you sit with thought leaders, authors, and trusted online educators and learn from their experiences.

Students on LinkedIn learning can take learning paths, taking courses to build their skills on a topic while growing from beginner to expert levels. Although LinkedIn Learning isn't free, many public libraries in the U.S. offer free access to its courses for learners with a public library card.

- **Udacity**

With a focus on data science, cybersecurity, AI, and other in-demand tech skills, Udacity exposes learners interested in entering the US tech industry via online resources.

Udacity breaks down learning into nano-degree paths that provide successful students with credentials. Udacity has free and paid courses. While all courses on Udacity are in English, others may be available for translation into other languages.

- **Other Memorable Mentions**

Yes, I know I said I'll tell you about my three favorite digital learning platforms. But I'd feel cheating you to explore other options and create *your* favorite list without mentioning other helpful digital learning platforms like:

- Udemy

- Adobe

- Small Business Administration

- OpenLearn

- Microsoft Learn

- edX

- Adobe

- Grow with Google

- HP Life

Networking without a Degree

Many young people who don't necessarily fancy a degree sometimes still want to go to college because they don't want to miss out on the social experience of college life. These folks feel that college allows you to network with great individuals and consequently boost your career prospects.

And they're not entirely wrong. College is where basketball games, frat parties, dorms with all sorts of people, and all other extra-curricular stuff happen. It can be a great place to meet friends and enjoy opportunities.

But it's definitely not the only – or best – way to build your network.

Horizontal and Vertical Relationships

While college lets you network with your colleagues, most of your college connections are within your age range. In other words, college mostly affords you *horizontal networks* where almost everyone is similar to you in demography. You're relating with teammates in the football team, music bands, or classmates.

However, age isn't the best default for grouping people with one another.

Your best growth potential actually comes from relating with people much younger and older than you (*vertical networks*). A vertical network lacks the demographical stereotypes you'll often find in college groups or teams, such as age, location, and gender.

Often, vertical networks include people who are very different from one another, save for one or two common interests. Compared to horizontal relationships, these kinds of relationships will benefit your career and financial goals in the long run.

It Doesn't Need a Fortune

Meanwhile, spending a fortune to get a social life or network is definitely not the best way to get social. It costs an average of living on campus at a public 4-year in-state college in the US $26,027. That's roughly $108,364 over four years!

There are plenty of other ways to build a quality network.

Other Ways to Build a Solid Professional Network

While college is a great place to build a network, the thousands of dollars it costs can be too expensive for *just that*. Here are other ways to expand your professional network for a fairer price.

1. Attending Conferences

Conferences are held all across the country for almost any interest you could imagine. These events have focused times on learning about a particular interest within a short time.

These conferences are also excellent for meeting exciting people who share your interests. You're more likely to meet people from all age backgrounds and have the chance to build your vertical network!

2. Engage in Social Networks and Groups Related to Your Interests

Join relevant LinkedIn, Facebook, and Reddit Platforms. GitHub communities and Twitter Chats are also excellent networking platforms.

Do you fancy music or philosophy? There are various social networks filled with people who love discussing exciting ideas.

Moreover, most professional businesses and brands now have some social presence. Network with organizations: social networking sites let you associate with specific organizations, connecting you with other like-minded individuals.

My point? There are hundreds of networking opportunities available on networks you already use. Take your profile seriously, share helpful content with your networks, and establish yourself as a valuable person in your field.

3. Find Exciting Things to Do in Your City

Volunteer at a library or any central location that allows you to meet with intellectual individuals excited about talking with a motivated and curious teenager.

By volunteering for causes you're passionate about, you can make dozens of helpful connections and establish yourself in that niche or industry. Volunteer in events like local festivals and musical events.

Also, consider becoming a tour guide in your city. That way, you can help meet people you would never interact with otherwise. You'll also get to know your city better as you discuss with people who have never been there.

4. Maintain Your Existing Relationships Courteously

After every meeting, coffee date, or call, send thank you notes to the other party. It could be via a quick text, email, or a postcard out of nowhere. Showing appreciation for little things will set you apart from others when it's time for a recommendation.

Workbook 2

Conduct an honest self-assessment, identifying your strengths, any areas you'd like to improve, and goals you aim to pursue.

Here's an example to guide you

Strengths: *I'm a quick learner with knowledge and experience managing a high school publishing team. I've also effectively trained others to write and self-publish at the organization. My strengths include problem-solving and critical-thinking abilities, and I have used them to brainstorm new content production and publication strategies that have exceeded the organization's expectations.*

Areas Needing Improvement: *While I'm great at writing, speaking publicly is challenging because I dread seeing my audience look dissatisfied with my ideas. I also need to be more vocal during meetings and when expressing* *my opinions publicly.*

Core values: *I value compassion for my team members and respect for all. I believe in treating everyone like family, always seeking their welfare as far as possible. I also have a strong work ethic that makes me work constantly to meet my goals and quotas. I'm not afraid to ask for help from my team mates and superiors.*

Goals: *I plan to improve my public and interpersonal skills by speaking up more during meetings. I'll clearly communicate my ideas.*

Achievements: *I doubled the organization's readership in twelve months. I published an editorial and ran a features column weekly, increasing awareness and reader engagement by at least 20% in the last six months of my stay at the organization.*

Now, it's your turn. What are your strengths, improvement areas, core values, and achievements? How do they show you your most probable career paths or comfort zones? Are there new strengths you can develop to boost your career prospects? Only you can know you best. However, asking one or two people around you what they think about your self-assessment results won't hurt. See you in the next chapter!

Takeaway 2

I've put up some key things to take away from this chapter before we call it a wrap and move to the final chapter in this book's first part. Here you go!

While the boat's rudder signifies our goals, the oars are the systems you put in place to ensure you meet your goals. The oars decide how far you'll progress.

Commit to one goal, and the rudder stays in place and keeps you moving forward. Flip in-between goals, and the rudder moves all around, making it easy to find ourselves rowing in circles.

Set SMART (Specific, Measurable, Achievable, Relevant, and Time-bound) goals.

Remote work can be a lifesaver during moments of recession or financial difficulty.

Spending a fortune just to get a social life or network is not the best way to get social.

Age isn't the best default for grouping people.

Your best growth potential actually comes from relating with people much younger and older than you (*vertical networks*).

Chapter 3

Building Skills for Success

The future belongs to those who learn more skills and combine them in creative ways
– Robert Greene

Skills and Experiences to Thrive

Developing Soft Skills: Communication, Leadership, and Problem-Solving

Soft skills are vital to succeed as a leader, employee, or teammate. Effective leaders apply soft skills to engage and inspire their teams openly and honestly.

Soft skills are also called people skills. Most employers look out for these skills during recruitment. Meanwhile, we gain or develop soft skills as we relate with colleagues, family, friends, and acquaintances.

There are many people skills to pick up through your life experience, like the way you:

- Make decisions

- Adapt to difficult situations

- Communicate and work with others

- Organize yourself

As you climb up the ladder in your career, you'll need your soft skills to increase your opportunities and advance into better opportunities.

The Three Front Spikes in a Teen Leader's Crown

Of course, there are several soft skills to develop. But because every teen has unique traits such as personality, training, or upbringing, they'd find some people's skills tougher to pick up than others.

And that's perfectly understandable.

For instance, someone who never had the chance to speak in front of more than five people might need more time to develop public speaking skills. Meanwhile, another teen who had ample time speaking before their colleagues might be inexperienced in handling crises or tough situations.

I hope you get that point. Yeah?

But some people skills are necessary for a successful career, regardless of your personality or traits. I call them the Three Front Spikes in A Leader's Crown – Your Crown.

You probably already guessed the three most vital skills to build a successful career correctly– Communication, Leadership, and Problem-Solving abilities.

Why You Need These Three Skills

You need communication skills at every stage in your career, from writing cover letters to drafting elevator pitches, dealing with clients, or caring for people.

Leadership skills aren't just for top management officials in Fortune 500 companies. Every teen requires some leadership skills to prove they can manage themselves and their workloads or responsibilities.

Besides proper self-management, an effective leader also demonstrates other qualities like time management, conflict management, and mentoring skills.

Of course, you already know the world has more than enough problems. Your potential employers, business owners, and clients *have* problems they want to solve.

Your problem-solving skills will help you deal uniquely with a customer's problem, ask the right questions to understand problems better or research properly to understand every situation.

Actionable Tips to Develop the Three Front Spikes on Your Crown

Improve your leadership skills by:

- ✓ Organizing a schedule with a timetable to manage your personal and official duties

- ✓ Teaching others, either in person or by creating instructional manuals, infographics, or videos to share with your family and friends

- ✓ Motivating others by organizing activities (fun or educational; formal, semi-formal, or informal) such as a quiz

- ✓ Attempting to resolve conflicts between friends or colleagues

How about trying these to improve your communication skills?

- ✓ Joining a sports team or creative arts club?

- ✓ Practicing both formal and informal phone/video calls

- ✓ Volunteer in an event that allows you to speak in front of others

To develop your problem-solving skills, consider:

- ✓ Keeping a journal that demonstrates your mindset and how you solve problems

- ✓ Playing logic puzzles and games

✓ Brainstorming and developing plans for problems around you

✓ Joining projects where you solve challenges with others as a team

Transferable Skills

One of the harsh realities of the pandemic is that it forced many to take up new careers. During this change, prospective employers want to know what skills applicants can offer. Here's where the need for transferable skills comes in.

Transferrable skills are proficiencies useful in various industries, jobs, or roles. That means, whether you stay in the same career or hop to another industry afterward, you'd have developed the right skills to thrive.

Developing industry-specific skills like coding, social media management, and baking are great. But one of the best things you can do for your future is to learn transferrable skills to remain versatile and adaptable to various paths.

For instance, an empathic graphic designer who communicates clearly with their teammates is likely more valuable than one who doesn't design well in a team. Here, empathy and effective communication are top transferable skills that differentiate both designers.

Fortunately, transferable skills are what every worker *should* gain from every leadership, employee, or entrepreneurship experience. Whether volunteering, interning, freelancing, or working from home, these skills you'd use – and would usually learn – in any professional setting.

By mastering these skills, you absolve your potential employer or mentors from worrying about training you on them. Aside from communication, leadership, and problem-solving skills, here are seven transferrable skills to learn and start making positive contributions to your teams.

1. Analytical Reasoning

While analytical reasoning is a part of problem-solving skills, it's best presented as a stand-alone skill. It's how you break down a larger challenge into smaller problems to identify an effective solution.

2. Critical Thinking

Also similar to problem-solving skills, critical thinking involves evaluating and interpreting information to make informed decisions. The decision could be a course of action, a judgment, or a conclusion.

Critical thinking logically studies and evaluates evidence to decide whether to take specific information as an opinion, an irrelevant fact, or an unavoidable fact.

3. Adaptability

Most (if not every) roles sometimes require adjusting workflows, due dates, or even job approaches. Sometimes, you might need to learn new skills to complete certain tasks. Demonstrating the ability to adapt to change shows you can work with various teams while maintaining a positive attitude to get tasks done.

4. Teamwork

Teamwork involves working together as a team with others to achieve a common goal. Your future employers, leaders, or even colleagues would love a team player, i.e., someone who makes conscious efforts to contribute positively to the team.

5. Attention to Detail

Paying attention to fine details means you notice virtually everything. It means you're going through projects with a laser-focused lens to ensure everything is correct without losing the tiniest detail. Having this skill means your potential employer or teammate can count on you to aptly deliver on tasks and catch errors before they cost the team.

6. Project Management

Project management skills help you effectively manage tasks from start to finish. They help ensure everything happens within time and adjust the timeline when things go outside schedule. You'll prove valuable to your future teammates, employers, leaders, and even followers by showing you can readily visualize what a project needs to be completed.

7. Relationship-Building

Building effective relationships is a key to building any successful company. Good relationships are why businesses, brands, and careers thrive. Teens with excellent relationship-building skills can better manage differences or conflicts and help parties arrive at a forward-facing solution.

Online Courses and Self-Paced Learning

When many people think of learning, they often imagine a brick-and-mortar classroom or a scheduled online training full of learners. But those are only two of several other learning models.

The next two sections show you how to leverage three learning models – online courses, self-paced learning, and open-source learning platforms – to upskill and boost your career profile.

One benefit of all three models is the flexibility they often provide learners. The average working professional is busy all week, sometimes juggling multiple jobs or roles. Even if you don't have a full-time job yet, chances are high that you are already too occupied to include a rigid learning routine in your present activities.

Here's why adopting self-paced learning can be an excellent way to keep learning while engaging in other life responsibilities.

Self-Paced Learning vs. Online Courses?

Self-paced learning is a type of training that lets users enroll in an online activity or course and go through the learning materials at their own pace. While there are other types of online training, like webinars and live virtual training, only self-paced learning allows you to run without an instructor's pace or schedule.

Benefits of Self-Paced Learning and Online Courses

1. No Set Schedule

Many teens want to enjoy studying or working remotely. Fortunately, many trainers want to train or run their teams remotely, too – and sometimes at the learners' pace. Self-paced learning lets you decide when you want to learn and how much learning you have the time to accommodate.

2. Less Pressure

Studies have shown that learning online courses at your pace can help learners retain more knowledge. In-person seminars and training can be more mentally and physically stressful since people are almost always around you.

Teens who are shy or introverted will often experience this pressure more, possibly leading to lower overall performance during training.

Moreover, not everyone is cut out for studying at specific times of the day. While some are better students in the day, others focus better at night. Self-paced learning can help you learn at your most productive times.

3. Improves the Effectiveness of Instructor-Led Training

Instructor-led training and webinars are great for engaging users in real time. However, self-paced learning can help you continue the learning experience after completing the webinars and instructor-led online courses.

So, suppose you took an instructor-led webinar that taught about operating heavy machinery. You can continue the training after the webinar by following up with a self-paced learning program.

Next, we explore open-source learning platforms and how they can contribute to gift you a wholesome learning experience that prepares you for a successful and rewarding career.

Leveraging Open-Source Learning Platforms

An open-source learning platform is a freely available learning management platform. Open-source learning platforms are excellent tools for teen leaders, employees, and entrepreneurs to improve their knowledge and skills.

While open-source learning platforms may not be free, they're freely modifiable and accessible. Besides helping you learn from others, open-source learning platforms can help you create learning platforms and private learning spaces to teach others.

Even more – the best open-source learning platforms have a supportive online community that lets you enjoy a shared learning experience with other learners worldwide.

What You Stand to Gain from Open-Source Learning Platforms?

Before I show you the top open-source learning platforms currently blazing the trail in the EdTech industry, how about I show you the unique benefits of leveraging these opportunities?

- **Mobile Learning**

Open-source learning platforms concentrate on providing responsive and user-friendly learning experiences optimized for mobile gadgets. They adopt responsive design principles for creating mobile apps and web-based platforms that allow you to access course materials and activities via smartphones and tablets.

- **Gamification**

Now, I know you've probably never heard of *gamification*. But you most likely have had favorite games you probably still love. Many open-source LMS platforms have included game-like (or gamification) elements to help you learn or retain what you learned.

- **Personalized and Adaptive Learning**

Open-source learning platforms offer you a personalized learning experience you can adapt to suit your unique needs. For instance, suppose you started learning a course on programming; some open-source learning systems will subsequently register your interests and recommend tailored content around programming to you.

- **Integration with Third-Party Tools and Standards**

Here's where users can bring on videos, tools, and other learning technologies you think will help make your learning easier. Many open-source platforms also integrate with content authoring tools, video conferencing platforms, and other learning technologies.

- **Accessibility and inclusivity**

Meanwhile, many open-source platforms place special emphasis on inclusivity and accessibility. That means, among other things, that learners with disabilities can also access and participate in their learning processes.

That said, while many options are available, here are the top open-source learning platforms to try your hands on and upskill to boost your career profile.

1. Moodle

Moodle is a community-driven open-source educational platform with users from around the world. One of the largest open-source teams in the world, Moodle offers users a full kit of features that students, entrepreneurs, and tutors benefit from.

The platform enjoys global support and a multi-lingual community of students. That means you can enjoy learning while exploring the value of open and collaborative systems.

Moodle has a mobile version you can readily access via Android or iOS devices. It also has an extensive Moodle plugins directory for themes, blocks, additional activities, and more.

2. Chamilo

Chamilo would appeal to teens interested in learning about technology tools and software. It was built to create a clear communication channel and a network of contributors and service providers in the software industry.

Chamilo lets you easily create valuable content on its user-friendly interface. The open-source platform also has an online community where users can leverage a corporate knowledge base or other one-on-one learning options. Lastly, Chamilo is mobile-friendly. That means you can choose your own pace and place to attend courses.

3. Open edX

With Open edX, you can access various course contents, their video and textbook contents, while monitoring your progress in the course. Open edX was created through a collaboration among edX, MIT, and Harvard.

Suppose you'd want to use the platform to coach others in a semi-formal setting as a teenwise leader who will someday train or influence others positively. Open edX lets you create custom course structures, grading policies, contents, and more.

Then, you have the discussion forum and wiki platforms where you can share knowledge or learn alongside other students and experienced members. Additionally, the community includes webinars, blog posts, and upcoming online events to train members on various topics.

4. Canvas

Canvas is an open-source learning management software that makes teaching or learning easy. Canvas is adaptable, reliable, and customizable to various learning needs.

Moreover, this learning tool has a user-friendly interface and features that save time and effort while improving your skills and resume. Canvas has a self-paced learning model that lets you improve your skills while handling other jobs or responsibilities.

What's more? Canvas has a user base of over 300,000 learners and experts involved in sharing, collaborating, and shaping the open-source software. Of course, you can also integrate third-party software to transfer information to or from Canvas.

5. LRN

LRN is a full-featured software that lets you develop (or access) web-based learning communities. Should you need to create a platform to share helpful ideas, you can readily customize your courses to fit your audience's unique learning goals.

Lastly, LRN has a user-friendly interface that lets you choose your preferred language, set the right time zone for your class, or add other custom portlets to your classrooms or personal portal layouts.

Still on skill acquisition, the remaining subsections in this chapter explore how to master technical skills, embrace lifelong learning, gain practical experience through an internship, and showcase your skills via a project portfolio.

I almost can't wait to receive your feedback on how this book has helped shape and transform your life and career. But you've got to learn and master the basics first – including all relevant technology skills.

Mastering Technical Skills in the Digital Age

Fine. I understand not every teen reading this manual wants a tech career. But technology has impacted every aspect of our world; thriving without embracing tech is practically impossible.

Tech skills are the competencies that help you interact with the virtual world around you. Acquiring tech skills makes you more appealing to employers, potential mentors, and clients.

They range from basic word processing skills to emailing and more complex skills like artificial intelligence (AI), audiovisual design or editing, and web design.

However, while you couldn't learn all tech skills at once, it'd help to choose on-demand tech skills and competencies to help you stand out from the crowd and advance your preferred career path.

Here are 7 top technical skills to master to stay competitive and stand out among millions of other teens worldwide.

1. Computer Skills

Computer skills refer to anything from mastering typing to using Microsoft Office or coding. Gaining proficiency in computer skills has been a must-have tool even for Gen Z, and your Gen Alpha doesn't have it any softer.

Gain a general knowledge of computer systems and become attractive to employers across various industries.

2. Data Science and Analytics

Data analytics and science involve analyzing, categorizing, organizing, and quantifying large data sets. You want to understand spreadsheets and related data software before learning data science or analytics.

Besides improving your resume and preparing for a tech role or career, learning data science or analytics can help you develop transferrable skills like logical, critical thinking, and organizational skills.

3. Audiovisual Editing and Design

Here, the student learns to conceptualize, produce, edit, and distribute digital video content across various platforms. Learning how to navigate audiovisual (AV) design software is key to securing jobs like web content analysis, AV project management, and AV architecture.

4. UX and UI

User experience (UX) and user interface (UI) roles allow you to concentrate on how visitors enjoy or consume a media or product. Both skills are very helpful in developing software, apps, social media accounts, and websites. The top prerequisite skills to master UX and UI design include graphic or visual design proficiency.

5. Digital Marketing

Thanks to the digital revolution in the Information Age, almost every business, brand, or cause has an online footprint. Digital marketing helps to promote brands, products, and services to drive consumer engagement, increase their clientele base, and generate more ROI.

Digital marketers use tech tools and strategies like video marketing, search engine optimization (SEO), content marketing, and analytics to reach consumers on devices like computers, mobile phones, and tablets.

Again, even if you don't eventually take up a career in digital marketing, the skill may help you promote your brand or find subtle applications in other fields.

6. Coding

Coding is a means of communicating between or among computer systems. It's the bedrock of most apps, web programs, and computer systems.

Suppose you haven't tried your hands on one programming language or another. Learning coding is often like learning a foreign language. Mastering it requires a significant amount of time and practice.

Computer scientists, programmers, app developers, and related careers all require coding skills. Popular programming languages include Python, Java, and HTML.

7. Artificial Intelligence

AI performs tasks that humans would usually do. It helps to increase the productivity, efficiency, and overall success rates of various processes.

Although it's an industry-specific skill, AI is becoming increasingly popular, and learning how to use AI tools will increase your chances of getting into various fields.

According to a 2022 Forbes report, AI will contribute up to $13 trillion to the global economy by 2030! Should you master artificial intelligence technologies like computer vision and automation, you're joining a very lucrative and productive industry.

Embracing Lifelong Learning and Continuous Improvement

Henry Ford founded the Ford Motor Company and was the Model T car inventor. His ingenious mind introduced the world to the moving assembly line method of car production.

By the mid-1920s, Ford had an estimated net worth of around $1.2 billion, registering him as one of the wealthiest Americans that ever lived. I'm not asking you to learn engineering or own a car company. Instead, I think a man who raised over $188 billion and left most of his wealth to a foundation is worth listening to, especially when he speaks about education.

Henry Ford once said, 'Anyone who stops learning is old, at twenty or eighty. Anyone who keeps learning stays young.' By that, he was advocating for a lifelong commitment to improving your skills and knowledge to stay relevant and valuable to the planet.

Now, I hope that isn't too harsh.

But you *probably* get my drift.

Besides helping you keep your brain strong and healthy, lifelong learning can improve your life satisfaction, optimism, and self-confidence. The drive to explore and learn new things can help you stay abreast of the latest developments in your field in a highly dynamic world.

And I won't forget that scientific research has shown that our brains have evolved to release 'good-feeling' chemicals like dopamine when you learn new things – like knowledge, information, skills, or just *about anything*!

Becoming Proactive About Lifelong Learning and Improvement

Most teens will pick up some new things during their daily routine. It could be something they heard someone say or do or something they found when surfing the net or reading a magazine.

However, that's effectively different from *trying* to learn something new. You want to be more proactive in learning something new about your career, personal life, or environment. And there's no better way to show that than creating an organized structure around learning.

Here are helpful tips to get you started.

- **Recognize Your Interests and Goals**

Remember, lifelong learning and improvement is about you, not other people or what they want for you. Reflect on your visions, passions, goals, or interests.

Whatever career or field you intend to grow in, here's the place to create a self-directed learning plan to accomplish the goal.

- **Create a List of Skills You'll Want to Learn**

Once you've identified your motivations, it's time to explore the skills to help you reach your goal. Create a list of soft and hard skills that are helpful to arriving at your destination. This list will help streamline your learning processes to a focused range of options.

Of course, that doesn't mean you completely ignore anything that seemingly doesn't fit your intended career path. (It won't hurt to tickle that dopamine effect even more!)

- **Embrace a Beginner's Mindset**

Embracing a beginner's mindset means you're embracing an attitude of openness, eagerness, and a lack of preconceptions. Besides making it easy to learn about new things, a beginner's mindset helps you stay curious. That way, you're better prepared to learn even more deeply about things you already know alongside a whole new world of possibilities or worldviews.

- **Learn, Unlearn, and Relearn**

Continuously learning and improving extends beyond discovering the latest news or the hottest skill on the job market. It also includes unlearning and re-learning things you already know.

Unlearning begins when you acknowledge that something you know is incorrect or obsolete. You wouldn't be the best fit for a driving role if you learned driving with 90's model cars any more than you would want to stay relevant without unlearning some things you've learned.

Unlearning should come before re-learning, which is how you update your knowledge or skill set to stay valuable to your world as it evolves.

- **Connect to a Community of Learners**

The lifelong learning journey won't be successful if you're going solo. It'd help engage with a community of learners through online platforms, educational institutions, or local meetups.

Connecting with a community of lifelong learners helps you exchange ideas, collaborate on projects, and gain insights from various perspectives. These connections can also foster a sense of support and belonging, inspiring you to continue your learning journey.

- **Make a Commitment**

Committing to never stop learning is the final and most critical step here. After setting realistic expectations on skills you intend to learn, commit to it and avoid making excuses.

Gaining Practical Experience through Internship

I couldn't say this enough – having a good degree is no longer the all-important requirement to secure the right jobs. In many unconventional roles, having the right experience is as valuable as, if not more important than, having a degree.

As a result, internships have become important to help teens and budding professionals stand out among their peers.

According to a survey by the National Association of Colleges and Employers Class of 2019 report, of the graduating seniors who received at least one job offer, 57.5% who had an internship had an offer, while 43.7% of graduating seniors who didn't have an internship didn't get an offer.

And you couldn't blame their employers. The practical experience from it reduces the amount of training they'd conduct to get the graduates job-ready.

What You Stand to Gain from Internships

Internships help you provide a valuable addition to any industry, career, or network you're interested in. During an internship, you'll usually get a placement in a company, often without pay or at minimum wage. Your highest reward from such ventures would be the industry experience that exposes you to the workforce.

A Possible Permanent Role

Many internships serve to introduce potential employees to the company. In many organizations, you can find and get placement in the organization after completing your internship as a regular staff.

Meanwhile, your internship also helps you make relevant connections with experienced people in your chosen field to widen your professional network. These individuals can be valuable in providing references and referrals when you're seeking other positions elsewhere or in the future.

Gaining Hands-On Industry-Specific Experience

Internships let you gain practical experience in your chosen field you may have learned or mastered when studying a skill. These skills could range from dealing with actual clients to juggling tasks from various superiors.

Internships can also show you how firms in your chosen industry work as you join in meetings and take on real-world projects.

Beyond Technical Skills

As you'd know by now, technical skills aren't the sole requirement for a successful career. Without soft skills, your technical skills risk producing results below their potential. You need people skills like collaboration, attention to detail, and working under pressure.

You're likely to face strict deadlines from your employer or team leader or have to work with someone with a different worldview from yours. An internship exposes you to the challenges of a work environment and gives you ample experience that can come in handy during future interviews or elevator pitches.

Gain a Competitive Edge

There may be thousands of other applicants like you for a role, contract, or audience. One way to maintain a competitive edge is by demonstrating your skills and experience by informing prospective employers of your internship experience.

Additionally, a history of internships shows that you have the drive and passion to seek experience outside just studying, not minding minimum wage (or no-pay) conditions.

Build a Strong Resume

Internships are excellent additions to your resume. Telling prospective employers or recruiters about your past internships shows you have considerable experience in the field and workforce.

Mind you, when listing an internship in your resume, indicate the specific skills or experiences you've gained. Mention specific processes, software, clients, or techniques you know. You may also want to include a list of your placement's highlights, as these can make very valuable points in your resume.

Showcasing Skills through Project Portfolio

Talking about building a strong resume – getting all the required skills and experience is unnecessary if you can't *show* it. A strong project portfolio of past works you've accomplished is how you convince your recruiter you know your opinions.

Depending on your field, a project portfolio might come in various forms. However, a project portfolio is essentially a visual representation of your accomplishments, skills, and experience. Potential clients or employers often critique your portfolio to assess whether you'll make a right fit for a role or contract.

Crafting a Project Portfolio That Sells

The perfect portfolio doesn't just include evidence of past projects you've done in a specific niche. It does it intriguingly and engagingly to sell your brand effectively.

Here are helpful tips to create a convincing project portfolio and improve your chances of landing a job, role, or professional relationship.

1. Write a Strong Personal Brand Statement

Also called an 'about me' statement or your 'bio,' a personal brand statement is an excellent way to introduce yourself, gain credibility, and instantly stand out.

Infuse your bio with your personality and unique voice, letting prospective clients know what you have to offer. Remember to include what sets you apart from others. Whether you're adding a short story, work history, background, or special experience, ensure that your personality shines through in your bio (and portfolio!).

2. Create a Visually-Appealing and Engaging Portfolio

Remember, your goal is to get your recruiter and potential employer to notice your work. One way to achieve this is by putting together a visually appealing portfolio.

Choose a subtle color scheme and layout that makes your work stand out without distracting the viewer's attention from the contents. Where applicable, ensure your portfolio is easy to navigate on mobile and tablet devices.

Another way to engage your audience is by using features like shapes, icons, animations, and video presentations. These can bring your portfolio to life, keeping your audience glued to the end.

3. Keep an Updated Portfolio

Your portfolio should never stop growing. Update your portfolio regularly with new and relevant projects. Meanwhile, if your portfolio contains links, check regularly to confirm all links are working and your copy is error-free.

Review your references and contact information. That way, you'll make it easier for prospective employers or clients to research about you or get in touch.

4. Highlight Relevant Achievements and Affiliations

Whether you're just starting on a skill or you've had a couple of experiences in the role, recruiters want to see you as a serious professional. One way to show that you take your job seriously is to include awards or recognitions on your portfolio site.

Showing these achievements can help to show how much you've fine-tuned your skills. Also, remember to put your best foot forward, highlighting your best strengths and competencies.

Do you have relevant Google certifications or industry accreditations? Don't leave them out. Include any industry affiliations you have to show that others also value your work and expertise.

5. Add Testimonials from Clients and Industry Experts

Marketing experts know that 'word of mouth' remains one of the best methods of advertisement despite the advanced tools and platforms available today. One of the best ways to show your competence is by including testimonials from employers, colleagues, or past clients.

Include LinkedIn recommendations and client feedback on your past work. You may also want to include testimonials from industry experts whose opinions are relevant to the role you're applying for.

If you don't already have them, consider asking for testimonials and client feedback to build social proof and trust with prospective employers. Suppose you're a baker applying for a full-time role at a restaurant. Consider including feedback from previous chefs you've worked under or links to online reviews from your past clients who were satisfied with your service.

Workbook 3

Use the lessons learned in this chapter to create a visually appealing and engaging portfolio.

After creating your portfolio, share it with a mentor or more experienced person in your field and get their feedback.

Review the feedback and make the necessary corrections.

Takeaway 3

I hope you've learned many things about building the right skills for a successful career in this chapter.

However, without filling you in with the information you already have, as you head to the next part, never forget this lesson on lifelong learning from Henry Ford.

Stop learning, and you immediately become old, whether you're twenty or eighty. Keep learning, and you'll stay young, agile, and always valuable to the world around you.

Part 2

Thriving Beyond Degrees

Whether it's Bill Gates, Michael Dell, or Steve Jobs, you've probably heard how these people became billionaires without college.

I'm not writing this book to discourage you from earning a degree if you have the resources to foot it. Steve Jobs, for instance, primarily left Reed College after spending six months on campus because he felt the cost was beyond him.

Instead, my goal in this book is to ensure you're confident and prepared enough for a successful career *beyond* degrees – whether or not you choose to go to college.

In this part, I share priceless career advice many adults wish someone told them when they were your age. Whether it's discovering the right job-hunting skills or learning rewarding financial habits, the life-saving lessons of this part are ones you don't want to miss.

They go beyond the basics of pursuing a great career, explained in Part 1, to handling some excellent tools and productivity hacks that can help you build a rewarding and fulfilling career.

Chapter 4

Conquering the Job Jungle

'Believe in yourself! Have faith in your abilities! Without a humble but reasonable confidence in your own powers you cannot be successful or happy.'

– Norman Vincent Peale

Standing out in the Job Market

Resumes That Stand Out

You've discovered the hidden potential in you via your interests and passions. Going beyond unearthing what makes you tick and *tick* others, you've taken the time and effort to build relevant skills for success.

Now, you're getting closer to your dreams – landing a dream job or opportunity you imagined while learning relevant skills or studying for this career. Your next job could be *the* big break in your career!

But you consider the competition in the job market – 'How do I stand out from these other applicants, even when some have more experience than I?' you're possibly asking.

Truly, you may be up against more experienced candidates. But you can perform better than them by creating a great resume.

Your potential employers want to hire the best applicants – and resumes are likely the first step in that search.

Why Create a Great Resume?

Employers look at resumes for an average of only six or seven seconds – and that's enough to impress or disappoint them. Submitting a weak resume can immediately remove you from the run.

According to Zippia research, professionally written resumes aren't just great for landing an interview but can also increase your earning potential by 25%. However, according to the online recruitment services company, the average job-seeker needs to send an average of 50 to 100 resumes before getting hired.

But the more impressive and professional your resume is, the less the number will be, and the less time you'll have to wait before getting a job.

Your resume is your first opportunity to prove yourself to your potential employer.

Use these practical strategies to make your resume stand out and demonstrate you're the best candidate for a role.

Personalize Your Resume to Match the Job's Requirements

Consider what your potential clients or employers want from the job description before drafting a resume. Then, personalize the resume to match the job's requirements.

Ensure your resume fits the company's culture and keywords. Prioritize employment experience that showcases relevant qualifications or skills. Suppose you're applying for the role of an HR intern, including skills you gained while leading a team in high school or judging an official contest among your colleagues would sound better than your cookery skills.

Include a Header and Summary or Objective

Just like your project portfolios, your resume needs a header that includes a summary of your bio or career objective. Ensure your header includes your name at its very top. Beneath the header should be your address (or just city and state), phone number, and email address.

Your bio comes right below your header. Keep it to a minimum of three sentences and a maximum of four sentences. A great bio helps prospective clients learn about you and your unique qualities that can help you stand out from the crowd.

Focus on Achievements, Not Just Duties and Responsibilities

Your potential clients or recruiters don't just want to read a list of your duties or official responsibilities. They want concrete examples of your achievements in past roles that depict your unique contribution to this new role.

That also includes sharing information such as awards you earned in high school or other quantifiable results that might impress your potential employer or client.

Quantify As Often As You Can

Writing about your previous experience will always help quantify your success in numbers. So, rather than say, for instance, 'My contributions at XYZ team helped us increase our clientele base, as my supervisor also confirmed,' how about:

'My supervisor noted that my joining the team brought and retained businesses worth $2 million over my six-month internship'?

Does that make any sense? Yes?!

Providing the right metrics can help to highlight your achievements more clearly and give the recruiter a clear sense of how you impacted your past employment. That way, they can better imagine what positive contributions you could bring.

Keep It Concise

While a resume can be two pages, keep yours to just one. As you draft your resume, it'd help only to share information that could help you stand out against the competition. No one wants to read about you and everything that happened since childhood.

Make It Visually Appealing

Avoid using unprofessional designs in the bid to beautify your resume. The key word here is *professional* aesthetics. Here are a few things to note when creating a visually-appealing resume.

- **Font:** Use legible font. Georgia, Times New Roman, Calibri, or Helvetica – and at size 12 – are great ideas.

- **Template:** Keep your designs minimal. If you're using a template, ensure the visual elements don't distract from your resume's contents.

- **Color:** Use an attractive color scheme when crafting your resume. Think black, white, and a third color, like green or blue. White is excellent for a background color, while black is best for your text. The third color can highlight important aspects of your resume. Consider keeping your resume's colors to no more than three.

Art of Job Searching

If you haven't heard this from anyone before, I'd take pride in being the first to tell you. 'Job-hunting is a part-time job in itself.' And many job seekers often don't get any real headway in their job search UNTIL they take it as a part-time (or full-time) occupation.

Now, there's no need to worry. Once you land the right job, you'll have all the time to concentrate on your career and other aspects of your life.

Your job search is dynamic and would often turn out to be a game of numbers. There are companies you really want to work for, and those closely match your profile. Some companies wouldn't hire you, and there are those you don't want to work for.

Guess what? Apply to as many companies as possible – or, if possible – everywhere! You often won't know which organization still has positions available or whether a cold mail conversation can actually turn into an actual job opportunity.

Moreover, should you get multiple job offers? Excellent – that gives you leverage to select and choose to taste.

Regardless of the industry or niche or industry you're working in, here are fundamental tips to guide your job search.

Throw Self-Doubt Out of the Window

Now, remember what I mentioned about applying *everywhere*? Yes, so many young people fall into the rut of thinking they aren't good enough for some jobs. They'd list a thousand-and-one reasons why they can't or shouldn't.

But you couldn't be far from reality if you give in to fear and self-doubt – two crippling factors that keep people from finding the jobs they really want.

Here's me saying,

'You can. And you should.'

I know the job search experience can be daunting. While some teens around you (or you) might get a little lucky without experiencing the hardship of finding a job, job hunting can be quite stressful for most people.

Eliminating self-doubt means staying positive on the role and following up on positions you applied to. It also means you treat your job search as a full-time role.

Then, you want to demonstrate focus by creating a system that tracks the positions you've applied to – say, an excel spreadsheet.

You're more likely to begin experiencing progress when you concentrate on the job search with enough determination and grit. As your progress starts from landing rare responses to landing job interviews, you'll start to see some light at the end of the tunnel.

And you can rest assured a little light is always better than outright darkness.

Develop a Personal Brand-Awareness

A great resume is important for convincing your employers to pay a closer look at your profile or application. But your resume might prove contradictory if you don't show your public profile matches the information on your resume.

Also called self-awareness, brand awareness is how people – including the hiring manager – perceives you via information you put in the public domain.

Whether it's your LinkedIn profiles or your social media accounts on TikTok and Facebook, you're always being judged without your knowledge.

Developing a personal brand-awareness means you control what people see or hear about you online. And most of this content comes from your handles.

What do your social media accounts say about your work ethic, experience, lifestyle, or interests? Begin a personal inventory of your personal brand to present the best image of yourself or your corporate brand to potential clients and employers.

Set a Job-Hunting Strategy

Create a schedule that best works for you to pursue your dream gigs. This could include a minimum number of jobs you want to apply to daily (or weekly).

Meanwhile, a holistic job-hunting strategy also includes a plan to learn *how* to apply for jobs. Read articles, watch videos, and enroll in courses that can help boost your success rate in your applications. Brush up your interview skills and get a few automated answers to specific questions your interviewers might ask.

Embrace the Good Side of Things

During the job-hunting journey, questions often go unanswered, and some things are completely out of your control.

But it doesn't have to be complex. Once you complete a list of tasks like brushing up your resume and auditing your LinkedIn and social media channels, ensure you have fun throughout the rest of the process.

You'd likely meet many new people who will become part of your professional network afterward. Sometimes, you'll find experienced professionals who wouldn't mind sharing unsolicited advice that can benefit your career.

And what if you don't get the role? You don't have to be discouraged. Rejections are part and parcel of the process.

While it's important to expect the best from your applications, accept that there are things you can't control. Meanwhile, many other applications could prove successful.

I can't stress enough how your personal life can affect your career. Ensure you live life without harboring negative or unproductive energies or habits. Embrace the good side of things and enjoy the rest of your teenage years (and life) to its *very* fullest.

Navigating Job Interviews

Navigating through various interview rounds is vital if you will get your dream (or preferred) job.

I'll let you in on some excellent interview hacks. But before that, let's run through the most common challenges people often face during an interview.

3 Common Interview Challenges

1. Nervousness

Feeling nervous about your next interview is normal, especially if your future career hangs on it. However, being excessively nervous can impair your performance.

Take a few deep breaths before heading into the interviewer's office. Refresh your mind on all the credible reasons why you should get hired.

It might also help to imagine you'll land the role regardless of what happens during the interview. Doing so can help you stay optimistic about the interview – and the entire application.

2. Tough Questions

Interviewers often include challenging questions in your interview process to test specific soft skills. When faced with a tough or tricky question, take some time to gather your thoughts before speaking.

If the question is long, answer each part separately to ensure you cover everything. Ask for clarifications if you don't understand the question. Meanwhile, be honest when you can't answer a question; avoid making up stories to *please* your interviewer. You could get caught up somewhere along the line!

3. Salary Discussions

Avoid asking questions about your salary expectations in the first interview – especially if the interview hasn't disclosed any information.

And when you eventually bring it up, it'd help to research the salary range for the role so you can set your expectations. Remember to consider your experience and qualifications while considering additional perks on the job before evaluating the pay.

7 Hacks to Ace Your Next Interview

1. Research the Company

You want to properly research the company you intend to work for – their mission statement, core values, work culture, and background. Doing so can help you understand what these organizations expect from their employees.

This knowledge can also help you tailor your answers correctly during the interview. According to a Glassdoor report, 79% of hiring managers expect applicants to research their company.

2. Practice Answers to Common Interview Questions

It's essential to practice your answers to common interview questions ahead of your meeting with the hiring manager. Often, hiring managers ask related questions like:

- 'Tell us your reasons for pursuing this role.'

- 'What are your strengths and weaknesses?'

- 'Provide case scenarios of when you faced and overcame specific work challenges.'

- 'Why did you choose our company (or brand)?'

- 'What are our mission statements, core values, etc?'

3. Dress the part

Dressing appropriately is vital to make a good first impression. You want to choose professional, neat, clean, and well-pressed clothes.

Different job roles might have unique outfits appropriate for an interview. It'd help to research ahead of what is acceptable in your industry.

Finance roles, for instance, might require a little buttoned-up appearance. Meanwhile, it'd be great to let your creativity show through a business casual outfit when preparing to interview for a tech opportunity.

Virtual interview? Choose comfortable clothing and double-check that your camera angle doesn't show any details you don't want the other person on the call to see.

In summary, find an outfit that makes you feel confident and comfortable – within acceptable boundaries.

4. Be Punctual

Plan to arrive at least 30 minutes before the scheduled time. Doing so will give you ample time to relax and compose yourself before the interview.

Avoid being late as that could negatively impact your time management and organizational skills.

5. Demonstrate Confidence

Maintaining eye contact is key to showing confidence. Sit up straight and speak coherently. However, avoid 'over-expressing' your confidence to avoid coming across as arrogant.

For instance, while maintaining eye contact, briefly look away from the interviewer and look back to affirm you're following the conversation.

6. Ask Relevant Questions

Interviewers often ask applicants if they have any questions. Here's your best – and possibly – final chance to showcase your interest in the role. Ask relevant questions that show you have researched the position and are genuinely interested in the role.

Doing this can also help you better understand the company's culture and conclude if this will make a right fit for your career.

7. Follow-Up

After the interview, it'll help to send a thank-you email or note. That will showcase your professionalism and keep you on top of your interviewer's mind. Don't hesitate to reiterate your interest in the role, and appreciate the interviewer for their time.

Building a Portfolio – Understanding Various Portfolio Types

In the last chapter of part 1, I showed you how to create a project portfolio. A well-crafted project portfolio helps your recruiter verify your competence and decide if you'll be a great fit for the role you're applying for.

Now, while every detail in that ending subsection in the last chapter will always help you build a convincing portfolio, they refer to only one portfolio type: the project (or showcase) portfolio.

The project portfolio also called the showcase, formal, or career portfolio, is helpful for teens with substantial work experience. It shows your best achievements, projects, or works.

However, what if you currently don't have work experience and need to show some *evidence* of competence, passion, and suitability for a role?

Here's where other popular portfolio types come in. Each of these other portfolio types can help you formally demonstrate your interest and potential abilities to function excellently in a role.

They include the:

- Process or learning portfolio

- Assessment portfolio, and

- Hybrid portfolio

Let's look at each of these other portfolio types and how they can help boost your application.

The Process or Learning Portfolio – I'm-a-Work-in-Progress

The process or learning portfolio is also called a development, reflection, or formative portfolio.

As the names suggest, this portfolio type depicts you as a work in progress, with high chances or stakes to complete a learning program or skill.

A process portfolio won't necessarily include your best work. Instead, it'll show your recruiter various learning attempts or unpolished documentation of your learning history. It also doesn't arbitrarily hide your challenges and struggles.

Suppose you're learning UX/UI design and want to apply for an internship role where you can perfect your skills on real-world tasks.

You haven't worked with a real client before, so wouldn't have a project portfolio. However, you've made several mock-attempts to reproduce various existing websites. Creating a learning portfolio of these mock-attempts showing your budding web design skills can go a long way to convince a recruiter that you're ready to learn.

There's a word of caution here, however. Avoid falling into the 'digital dump' trap.

The digital-dump trap makes learners or budding professionals include lots of *artifacts* and irrelevant information in their portfolio. It makes your portfolio (or your personality) come across as disorganized or purposeless.

You want to demonstrate your learning process in an organized and meaningful manner via your I'm-a-Work-in-Progress-but-I'll-Get-There portfolio.

Assessment Portfolio

The assessment portfolio is often used in educational or training systems. They go beyond showing the details in the learning portfolio to show that you've mastered various curriculum elements.

Think of an assessment/accountability portfolio as your SAT (or GCE if you live in the UK). It shows your teachers (and possibly your recruiters) that you're due or qualified for a certification or degree.

Let's look again at the web design learner illustration I used when describing the process portfolio. The web designer-in-training has now completed their course and *feels* competent enough to work with little (but necessary) supervision on projects.

Rather than show rough mock-ups of real-world websites they've created, you want to submit clean replicas of others' work with possible video snippets that confirm you actually worked on the project. There is little or no room for rough edges or disorganized presentations here.

Remember, your goal is probably convincing them enough to give you a trial and eventually hire you. Put your best foot out and show you're ready for a real-world role.

The Hybrid Portfolio

The hybrid portfolio would combine some or all portfolio types – the showcase, process, and assessment portfolios.

Consider creating a hybrid portfolio to demonstrate various skills and proficiencies in your portfolio. Remember, you want to show yourself as being a valuable or potentially valuable asset to your prospect.

That means your hybrid portfolio could include, for instance, information on skills you've already perfected or even sold (showcase).

It could also highlight skills you're learning, demonstrating how they can help enhance your value to the organization or role. Without including unnecessary details about *everything* you've ever learned, a hybrid portfolio dynamically highlights your current and potential competencies.

Freelancing and Gig Economy

The world is entering a gig economy, where more organizations shift toward hiring staff on a contract basis. Many contract staff work as free agents and remote workers rather than full-time or part-time permanent employees.

Perhaps no other factor has contributed to the growth of the freelancing economy like the pandemic. Today, over a third of US workers – around 57 million people – are engaged in the gig economy. Experts predict that number will grow to 87 million by 2027.

That tells you, among other things, that the future looks positive for freelancers – and for you if you choose to take this path.

Sadly, the gig economy has received some negative reputation lately, especially for fostering unhealthy work practices or little job security. However, it could amaze you to know that almost 60% of gig workers are in tech, design, and IT jobs. Another 24% have marketing, multimedia production, and content writing jobs.

Freelancing – The Catch, The Drawbacks

While freelancing and the gig economy's flexibility are valuable, many freelancers face a few hurdles.

Let's see some of the biggest advantages of freelancing.

1. **Flexibility**: Freelancing lets you fit your schedule around other factors like vacation and other creative passions. Often, freelancers also have the liberty to choose when they'll complete a task – a luxury that traditional roles hardly provide.

2. **Work without limits**: Freelancers can potentially work without any geographical boundaries. They're not limited to walk-in offices they commute to every morning. (However, some freelancers sometimes create offices to help boost their efficiency or productivity. But it's still subject to *their* choices anyway.)

3. **Liberty to choose your clients and projects**: Freelancers can choose projects and clients that align with their interests. This freedom provides an excellent medium to help you achieve your professional or personal goals.

4. **Increased earning potential**: Depending on your industry and expertise, freelancing can help you earn more than you would working in a traditional role. An increased earning potential also means you can earn income from various sources. For instance, should you lose one project or client, there are several others to fall back on.

Now, let's see some downsides to freelancing and how to beat these hurdles should you choose this career path.

1. **Lack of financial stability**: New freelancers often find it challenging to get a stable income stream. One way to avoid this is to start freelancing part-time and transition into full-time freelancing when you've attained some level of reputation and stability.

   Meanwhile, even established freelancers may see their finances fluctuate since they don't have a definite paycheck. But that's also the same story with business owners and many other career paths.

   To avoid this, consider putting aside a sufficient emergency fund and plan toward expenses like retirement savings, healthcare, and taxes. Understanding your financial stability can help you navigate the various income situations that may come with the gig economy.

2. **Work-Life Balance**: Full-time freelancing can be lonely at times or filled with other unhealthy work practices like overworking oneself. Since

freelancers don't have a traditional working environment, they often grapple with an inherent lack of social interaction.

One way to overcome this tendency is networking and engaging with other industry professionals, freelancers, and potential clients. Joining online communities or forums or participating in in-person industry events can also be helpful. Lastly, deliberately take time out to spend with friends and family.

3. **Staying disciplined and motivated**: Freelancers are generally solely responsible for their success. Cultivating self-motivation while maintaining a high accountability level (to peers, co-workers, or supervisors) is essential to keeping your morale and progress rate on point.

4. **Building a Client Network**: Building a lasting client network can help create a foundation for a steady work follow and a successful freelancing career. However, finding long-term clients may be challenging.

To overcome this, consider developing a marketing strategy that helps you establish a solid client base – and that could include creating a professional portfolio or website. Moreover, it'd help create strong relationships with existing clients and leverage referrals to increase your chances of retaining clients or gaining steady work.

Fortunately, the flexible economy has grown beyond just freelancing and the gig economy. Some companies also provide flexible working opportunities to their staff to attract a global pool of talent.

That way, they can avoid the limitations of a local talent pool and reach out to qualified hands willing to work.

Leveraging Social Media

Lastly, I'll show you how to maximize the power of social media to stand out in the job market. The clear and actionable hacks I'll present here are tested and proven tips that affirm that success – in any field, including yours – is never an accident.

Regardless of where you are now or where you're from, you can harness the power of social media to enhance your personal brand and increase your chances of succeeding in ANY career.

Enjoying the full rewards of a social media branding campaign won't happen overnight. Yes, it might take some years. But after a while, the results trickle in and motivate you to increase the intensity of your social media presence.

(Guess what? It could happen sooner than you expected, too!)

Here you go!

My 7 Productivity Rules to Leverage Social Media and Grow Your Personal Brand

1. **Understand Your Audience**: The first rule to grow your social media presence toward advancing your career is understanding your audience or market. The clearer you are about your target audience or market, the better you can appeal to them.

    It includes knowing, for instance, the age, sex, languages, and preferences of your potential audience. Once you've got this settled, you're ready to apply other productivity rules.

2. **Develop a Social Media Strategy**: Developing a popular or strong social media profile takes time and effort. But it also takes planning. Here's the time to develop an effective strategy that shows how you intend to achieve your personal branding goals. For instance, are you leveraging influencers, regular postings, or ads? What type of content are you posting? And the likes.

3. **Quality over Quantity**: Regarding content creation to drive traffic and followership, value quality over quantity. You want to target each post

or content to your audience or market, relaying a unique or important message every time. It's often difficult for people to reject or ignore valuable content.

4. **Follow High-Profile Accounts**: One way to increase your chances of building a high-profile account is to follow other high-profile accounts. Following high-profile accounts and engaging their posts can help create visibility for your brand. It can also help you see what tips or hacks seemingly work for those who have already mastered their craft.

5. **Engage Posts on Your Accounts**: Genuinely like, comment, and share posts on your account as often as you can. That way, you'll build relationships with others with time and increase the chances of building a loyal following. Of course, it won't happen overnight. But if you don't give people your time, expecting them to give you theirs might be quite *ambitious*, especially when you're yet to gather a large following offline or elsewhere.

6. **Avoid Promoting Always**: Using ads and other techniques to promote your contents can distract you from providing real value to your audience. Instead, spend time creating value without trying to sell something to them at every bend or turn. Promoting often could put off your existing or potential audience.

7. **Leverage the Power of Other Influencers**: A cheap way to get an influencer's attention to your account is by mentioning how they've influenced or inspired you. You could create content (in the form of videos, for example) that appreciates a role model for their work in a field.

If your profile syncs with the influencers' follower base, you might just gain some of their followers yourself. Many brands and newcomers to the social media space often use this approach early to drive engagement to their accounts.

Where there are enough funds, companies often pay influencers to advertise them. But you only need this when you have a budget for it.

Workbook 4

Audit your social media handles using the tips in this guide to ensure they contain only information you want your potential recruiters, clients, and coworkers to see.

Then, plan a social media personal brand development strategy toward growing your network and following and building the right platform for a successful career.

Takeaway 4

This chapter has so many takeaways I'll want you never to leave behind as you seek to excel beyond degrees.

1. Make your resume:

    - Visually appealing

    - Personalized to match the job requirements

    - Focused on achievements, not just duties and responsibilities

    - Include as many metrics as possible

    - Contain only relevant information

2. A job search requires as much effort as a full-time job to give you the best chances of landing your dream client, job, or relationship.

3. It's okay to be a little nervous or scared before an interview – most people are. But properly researching the company and demonstrating

confidence and a sense of responsibility or passion for the role can increase your success chances in any interview.

4. Even if you don't have a project portfolio, your learning portfolio or assessment portfolio might suffice to earn you a placement. Better yet, a hybrid portfolio showcases all your existing and in-the-works skills to your recruiter.

5. Never underestimate the power of social media to define or advertise your personal brand – whether or not you know it.

See you in the next chapter, where I will take you through a journey into financial literacy many grown-ups wish they had when they were your age.

Chapter 5

Financial Wisdom for Teens

'We were not taught financial literacy in school. It takes a lot of time to change your thinking and to become financially literate.'
– Robert Kiyosaki

Becoming Financially Literate

Creating and Sticking to a Budget

You probably already read the opening quote by Robert Kiyosaki, author of *Rich Dad, Poor Dad*.

Among many other vital lessons Robert taught on financial literacy, the best-selling author on financial intelligence explained that mastering finances would not happen overnight.

Whether creating a budget, sticking to it, building long-term investments, or understanding debts and loans, Robert would have you give it time.

However, you won't master any skills, including financial literacy, unless you start learning and practicing it anyway.

If you've not read any of Robert's books, I recommend reading at least one of his materials to any teen or young person wanting to build a financially secure future.

Let's begin our lessons on the basics of financial literacy in this chapter by explaining how you can physically set up a budget and stick to it.

Creating a Budget You Can Stick To

Some people are afraid to begin budgeting because they're afraid it'll be challenging. However, creating a budget is as easy as these five steps.

1. Define Your Income

Budgeting begins with your entire income. That includes any allowances, paychecks, and extra income from your account via side hustles, gifts, or freelance work.

2. List Your Expenses

To list your expenses, start with essential needs like savings, food, utilities, housing, giving, or transportation. Then, head on to other fun activities like restaurants, entertainment, and the like. Meanwhile, you also want to include the big expenses you're saving up for.

3. Budget *Everything*

Budget every income that comes into your account into giving, saving, or spending. Financial literacy experts call this form of budgeting zero-based budgeting or budgeting to zero.

Without leaving any room for unbudgeted income, this means listing all your expenses, subtracting them from your income, and converting all that's left into your current money goals (savings).

4. Track Your Expenses

Tracking your every money you spend is important. Log every expense in the correct section of your budget. That way, you can monitor your financial journey and increase your chances of sticking to the plan.

5. Budget Each Month Before It Begins

Budgeting before each month begins can help you better prepare for each month. Thinking ahead of every month increases your chances of remembering everything to include in your budget– and following it.

Sticking to Your Budget

You have financial goals and career goals that need funding. However, your budget won't do any good if you create one and then ignore it. You want to keep at your budget and stay with it. Here are a few actionable but powerful tips to stick to your budget every month.

1.   Cut Down on Big Purchases

If it's not necessary, take some days to consider it. You want to ask helpful questions like, 'How will this affect my savings?' 'What impact will it have on my daily expenses?' 'Is the benefit worth the cost?'

Doing this helps you include only expenses that add *value* to your life without *stressing* your budget. One excellent way to weigh how valuable a likely expense would be is to take a week to ruminate on it.

If you've forgotten it after a week, that's a good sign that you probably never needed it.

2.   Never Spend Money You Don't Have

While I'll treat understanding debts shortly, it's worth mentioning a thing or two about it here. Taking debts can lead to a vicious cycle that's difficult to escape. You'd often spend more on interest than you'd need if you had saved up or avoided the expenses.

Make a culture of postponing purchases you want to make for a week or month. Have you found a gadget, vacation, or course you want to pay for? Plan toward it. Rather than take a loan for it, save regularly toward it so you don't get thrown off your budget.

3.   Maintain a Grocery List

Sticking to a grocery list and planning your meals is one of the most straightforward and effective ways to save money and maintain a healthy budget. Plan your needs for the week without purchasing foods that will end up in the garbage unconsumed.

Thankfully, maintaining a grocery list will possibly help you eat healthier, too. It'll reduce your chances of purchasing junk that shouldn't fit into your meal plan. That leads us to the next savings tip.

4. Shop for Groceries Online

Shopping in walk-in supermarkets has a downside: You'd likely sneak a lot of $2 - $5 extras you don't need into your cart. And if you're hungry and have to shop for long hours? You might end up spending way more than your budget before returning home.

Shopping for groceries online can save you lots of time and reduce your chances of making spur-of-the-moment purchases. Create a grocery list to guide your spending online. Even more, when an item seems to cut beyond your budget for the week, you'll do well to save it toward future visits and keep your grocery budget consistent.

5. Pay Yourself FIRST

By asking you to pay yourself first, I'm not asking you to purchase that item you've always wanted since the last payday. I mean *putting money into a savings account* every payday before you make any other expenses.

Little payday savings can grow into something larger, which can eventually purchase that bicycle, pay for that emergency spending, or even purchase a house someday! Setting up automatic transfers can help you put yourself – and your future – first beyond any other expenditure or person.

6. Go on a Spending Freeze

A no-spend challenge involves committing to not spend money on anything that's not necessary. Consider going on a spending freeze for a week, a month, or even an entire year.

I understand it might appear intense. But it's a highly effective way to cut your spending habits and change your mindsets around money.

To start your no-spend challenge, write items you consider necessary and how long the challenge would take. And if you want to make it more fun? Challenge your friends or siblings to see who saves the most.

Like learning any other skill, financial literacy skills like frugality and savings are better learned with others.

7. Cut Down on Fees

I understand you care about watching your favorite TV heroes on Netflix or subscribing to listen to your favorite music on Spotify or Apple Music. However, several $10-a-month fees can quickly add up and impair your accounts in the long run.

How much goes into your monthly banking fees? Consider reducing the number of transactions you process to help reduce your monthly banking fees.

Now, all these fees might appear little and negligible. But living frugally is an art that grows into every other aspect of your expenditure.

Understanding Credit, Loans, and Debts

Credit, loans, and debt are three words you'll often hear along the same conversation lines. However, they're slightly different from one another.

While a loan gives you an amount you owe (debt), your credit shows how much you can borrow. I'll show you how both credit and debt work and how managing both can help you avoid financial trouble.

What Is a Credit Report and How Does It Work?

Your credit report is a document that shows your debt history over the last seven or more years. Potential creditors will often look at your credit report for a snapshot of your use of credit cards or loans.

Beyond your loans, your credit report could also include non-debt-related bills such as your unpaid utilities and rent. A typical credit report includes the following information:

- **Personal Information:** Your name, date of birth, SSN, previous employers and phone numbers

- Credit card account balances, limits, and information on whether or not you fulfilled the minimum payment each month.

- **Collections:** Bills and debts you couldn't pay that are purchased by debt collection agencies. This section would also include the collection agency's contact information and the amount you owe.

- **Loans:** How much borrowed initially, how much you owe, and your entire monthly payment history.

- **Inquiries:** The names of organizations that have requested your reports to pre-screen you or determine if you qualify for a new loan.

Usually, your credit report would include a credit score that summarizes your negligence or commitment to settling your debts on time.

Credit vs. Debt vs. Loan

Credit gives you the chance to make a purchase now and pay afterward. A debt, on the other hand, is how much you owe.

Here are examples that should completely clear your understanding of all three terms.

Suppose you have only one credit card you haven't used yet. You have credit but don't have any debt. But when you make a $200 purchase on the credit card, you become $200 in debt.

Meanwhile, you have debt as soon as you receive a loan. If you get a loan for $10,000, your initial debt is also $10,000, plus other fees you owe the lender.

What Is My Credit Score When I've Never Taken a Loan?

Chances are you haven't taken any credit or loan before now. However, there's no such thing as a zero credit score. If you've never used a credit card or taken out a loan, you likely don't have a credit score.

Why Your Credit Is Important

Your credit report or score can directly influence whether or not you get a new apartment, buy a home, save, or facilitate some important transactions.

Whether you're taking a mortgage or car loan, pursuing affordable car insurance rates, opening a utility account in your name, or renting an apartment, your potential lender would most likely review your credit report. Meanwhile, some employers also check your credit score when considering you for a role.

Of course, having bad credit doesn't mean you can't achieve any of the things I listed above, but it *makes it more difficult*.

How Debts Work

Mortgages, auto loans, and personal loans are popular debt examples. Usually, in most loans, the borrower receives money they must fully repay by a specified date, months, or years away. As a reward for their services, the lender charges an interest from the borrower, usually a percentage of the loan amount.

Unlike debts, credits have no fixed repayment date. The borrower has a credit limit that determines how they can use their credit card – as long as they don't exceed that limit. As of 2023, federal student loans for undergraduates usually come with an interest rate of 4.99%.

Suppose a student took a federal loan to pay for their college education. They'll receive some money they'll agree to pay back with interest.

Often, the government student loan would offer the student various repayment plans. A standard payment plan, for instance, would mean they'll make fixed monthly payments for 10 years. After that period, their debt *should* be completely paid off.

Different Types of Debts

Debts come in various forms, such as:

- **Collateralized debt:** You often pledge something valuable the lender could take should you fail to pay the loan.

- **Unsecured debt:** It doesn't require any collateral as security. This debt type is usually based on the borrower's creditworthiness.

- **Resolving Debt:** This offers the borrower a line of credit that limits how much they can borrow if they so wish. If the credit line says a maximum of $100,000, for instance, the borrower can take up to $100,000, repay, and borrow up to it again – as long as they fulfill their monthly payments.

- **Mortgage:** A mortgage is a form of secured debt used to purchase real estate and is usually repaid over long periods, such as 15 or 30 years. Besides student loans, mortgages are the largest loans consumers will ever get.

Paying Off Your Debts

Ever heard of good and bad debts?

Well, good debts involve taking debts to purchase assets (possessions that bring in further money). And credit cards could save a life during emergencies. However, debts can also be risky for both borrowers and lenders.

For instance, consumers could amass unimaginable debt if they lose their jobs or face some serious setback. Ultimately, this affects the debtor's credit score and reduces their chances of getting further loans.

The best way to plan to pay off your debts quickly is to devote much of your income to monthly debt payments. You want to offset credit card debts in full each month before any interest charges kick in.

That way, you can learn better debt management – and, with time, possibly stay debt-free.

Investing in Long-Term Financial Security

While you're learning better debt and credit management, here's a long-term strategy to become financially buoyant in your career.

While some investment choices can allow you to revoke your investments and rewards within a few years, investments are typically meant for the long haul. Successful investing goes beyond throwing money at stocks, bonds, or a mutual fund.

Meanwhile, it's not too early to begin saving toward profitable investments.

Long-term investing refers to investments that mature in at least five years. Here are five helpful investment tips you should know.

Investment Tip 1: Understand Your Financial Situation

The first thing to do to invest in the long term successfully is to know how much money you have to invest. Take stock of your assets and debts and devise a reasonable debt resolution plan.

Once you have these in place, you can fund long-term investments without running to recover your investments for a while.

You probably already know why that's wrong. Withdrawing funds early from your long-term investments reduces your goals, cuts your potential interests, and possibly forces you to sell at a loss. Of course, you might also incur expensive tax costs while cutting an investment before the expected dates.

Investment Tip 2: Understand How Much Time You Have

Different people invest for different reasons, from paying rent to funding a startup or mortgage down payments. Whatever your intention, ensure you understand how much time you have before you'll need the money.

That way, you'll know the best assets to invest in and how much risk you can take. For instance, if you're investing toward a company or a home you intend to purchase ten years away, you might be able to afford more risks.

Investment Tip 3: Understand Investing Risks

Here's where you need to understand the risks inherent in various investment portfolios. That way, you can avoid spontaneously reacting to every dip or rise in the market.

Generally, stocks are riskier than bonds, and cryptos are riskier than real estate. But even within riskier asset classes like stocks and cryptos, some investments are riskier than others.

For instance, US bonds are less risky than bonds issued by other less-developed nations. That's because less-developed countries often grapple with economic instability and unpredictability.

Mind you, assessing investing risks goes beyond assessing the credit ratings of different portfolios. There's something called *your* risk tolerance – and you must consider it before embarking on an investment journey.

Your risk tolerance level refers to how much risk you can take. Not everyone is cut out for heavy risks. Not everyone can watch the value of their investments go up and down without losing their sleep.

Investment Tip 4: Diversify

Another vital tip to successful long-term investing is spreading your portfolio across various assets. Doing this can help you increase your chances of 'winning' at any time throughout your long investing time frame.

Avoid diversifying into two or more highly similar investments or move in the same direction (such as REITs and real estate crowd-fundings).

It'd help to diversify your investment in various directions. A good place to start would be a mix of stocks and bonds. However, you can also diversify across large, medium, and small company stocks.

While you might not have all the technical knowledge about diversification, options like mutual funds and exchange-traded funds were created to help you diversify your assets. They help you easily build a diversified portfolio exposed to hundreds of individual stocks, bonds, or other related assets.

Investment Tip 5: Review Your Strategy Regularly

While you already made an investing strategy you'll stick to, it'll help to check in and make revisions periodically. For instance, review your strategy twice yearly to ensure your portfolio is still performing as expected.

Also, consider changes in your living conditions. A financial plan is an extension of your life. Things can happen suddenly, and they can justifiably impact your strategy.

Did you have a financial break? Is there a reason to increase or cut the investments? Reviewing your living conditions and the situation of your portfolio can help you have a successful long-term investing experience.

Building Emergency Funds and Savings

Whether you're 12 or 20 – you probably already know that life usually is filled with highs and lows.

Think of your emergency fund and savings as a shock absorber to help you navigate life's bumps and downtimes. If you still have a hard time wondering what a life bump looks like – COVID-19 is probably the best example to show you how impactful having an emergency is during a crisis.

Since you probably already understand why you need an emergency fund, let's dive into all the details about how to build an emergency fund effectively.

What Will It Cost You?

Reserving up to one-quarter of your annual earnings is a great idea and vital to building an effective financial plan. However, it will require some effort from you – that begins with you outlining how much you spend every month.

But you might be wondering, 'Why do I need to keep as much as 25% of my earnings in an emergency fund I might *never* touch anytime soon?'

I understand you probably have lots of things you'd love to spend on. And your income already feels slim.

However, today's economy is more uncertain and volatile than it has been. Besides, it's no longer the Industrial Age where corporate loyalty was an *in-*thing. You don't want to be caught unawares because you abruptly lost a job or role.

Even without global financial or health crises, emergencies like sudden illness or disability, major automobile repairs can be expensive. There's never a safe time for an emergency expenditure.

Meanwhile, putting aside just two or three months of expenditure is a small amount compared to what you'll need over the next 40 years.

Remember, a journey of a thousand miles begins with one step. If you don't take the first step now in a few months' savings, rushing to cover a thousand miles later in life would cost MORE.

Where to Put It

Money market funds and high-interest savings accounts are other excellent places to place your emergency fund.

Banks insured by the Federal Deposit Insurance Corp (FDIC) or the National Credit Union Administration (NCUA) are excellent options.

Online-only banks are also excellent options for saving toward emergencies because they often promise higher yields and lower fees than brick-and-mortar banks. Consider safe and *liquid* options that allow you to access your money when needed.

It'd also help to compare various options – their savings rates and account features before you eventually select a fund to work with. Look out for lower fees and costs.

The right choice will make it harder to dip into your investment – and reward you a little for leaving it for a while.

Acting out Your Plan

Buying less-expensive jewelry, clothing, or automobiles the next time you're shopping is an easy way to come up with some money for your emergency fund. There's nothing harmful in downgrading your cell phone service or cutting down the two-week vacation to a three-day visit. Save your next raise, bonus, or unexpected gift.

Eat at home instead of dining out often. Put 'cashback' and tax refunds into your fund. Think of it: put aside $5 a day to your fund, and you'll have $3,650 at the end of the year. That's $10,325 in ten years.

The key to successfully acting out your plan is regularly adding to the fund. Treat your fund like any other recurring bill you have to pay every month. Dedicate a section of your paycheck and set it aside.

Remember, you'll do well to 'pay yourself first,' not even credit card companies or your landlord. And that '*you*' includes your emergency fund.

Starting a Side Hustle

What came to your mind when you turned the chapter and read, 'Financial Wisdom for Teens' as the topic of this chapter? Perhaps you were already getting ready to learn the biggest money-making hack or idea – or some tip on starting a side hustle.

But your journey into financial independence won't begin until you understand the basics of budgeting, debt management, investing, and keeping an emergency fund.

Once you get the basics of financial planning right, you're ready to pursue income streams that produce the money you budget, save, or invest.

And I admit, the last few sections probably had so many technicalities you were almost tempted to skip through the pages.

This time around, you won't be hearing too many financial registers. Instead, I'll show you 21 trendy and profitable side hustle ideas to try in 2023.

Fortunately, you can start one or two of these side hustles on a part-time basis, charging your clients hourly. As your income increases, you can scale up your side hustle and turn it into a full-fledged business.

Here you go!

21 Profitable Side Hustle Ideas for Teens in 2023

Monetizing YouTube Channels

With over 2 billion users who watch 250 million video hours daily, YouTube has a high profit potential. Admittedly, it could take some time to get an audience large enough to help you profit from YouTube ads. But there are many other ways to make money on YouTube without paid ads.

Begin by producing great content that resonates with your target audience. As your following increases, consider introducing paid subscriptions or doing paid sponsorships.

Digital Marketing

Digital marketers help brands manage their online presence. They're often responsible for creating Google or Facebook ads, developing email marketing campaigns, or creating SEO content.

Tutor Online

Do you like working with kids or mentoring less experienced folks? Tutoring might be your thing. Fortunately, various online platforms are willing to pay anyone who wouldn't mind sparing a few hours weekly to teach a subject.

Deliver Packages

Delivering packages takes little or no technical skill. With Amazon Flex, you can sign up to deliver packages during your free time and earn extra income. Fortunately, work scheduling is flexible; you can sign up for a specific block of time and receive as many or as few delivery assignments as you have time.

Social Media Management

Social media managers help brands create and manage their social media presence. That could include tasks like setting up calendars, writing copies, developing strategies, and more. Brands often hire them as part of their marketing plan – and will pay them for their expertise.

Web Design

Web designers often have a user experience (UX) or user interface (UI) background. They help to ensure websites are beautiful and usable.

Web Development

Web developers are responsible for coding and configuring websites' back-end and front-end functionality.

Bookkeeping

Bookkeeping involves balancing checkbooks and reconciling financial statements or budgets for businesses.

Photography

Most weddings, birthdays, and dinners occur on weekends. You can run a successful photography business while still working full-time or studying on weekdays. If you prefer selling your photos, sites like Burst, Shutterstock, and Getty Images are always seeking to purchase photos to use on their websites or adverts.

Graphic Design

If you learned graphic design, consider selling your skills on websites like Upwork or Fiverr. Conversely, you can create designs for clothes, stickers, and other products and send them directly to your clients on Redbubble or other marketplaces.

Writing

Do you love writing? There are several ways to earn money as a writer. They range from writing for traditional publications and blogs, creating copies for marketing agencies, or reviewing resumes for job seekers. Platforms like Upwork or Fiverr also have gigs for various writing niches.

Lawn Care

For teens who may enjoy mowing lawns, people will gladly outsource their lawn mowing to others. With a couple of clients, you might soon run out of time in your part-time schedule and refer potential homeowners to others.

Baking

Baking would require you to meet up with state or national regulations. But if you love baking, it might be worth updating your kitchen enough to start selling food part-time.

Reselling Vintage Clothing

When Amoruso started reselling vintage wear at 22, she possibly never knew it would become the multi-million-dollar brand it turned out to be in ten years. You can turn your love for shopping into a side hustle by reselling clothing items you find at your local thrift shops.

Like Amoruso, you can create an online vintage store site like Shopify, eBay, or even Instagram.

Offer Pet Sitting and Dog Walking Services

People today tend to treat their pets like family, creating a growing demand for dependable hands to care for their furry friends. With apps like PetBacker, PetSitter.com, Rover, or Wag! it's way easier to find clients needing a pet sitter than ever.

Paid Online Surveys

Many researchers and companies would pay people to hear what they think about their products or services. Websites like Swagbucks, BrandedSurveys, and SurveyJunkie have tons of paid surveys.

App Testing

App testers help businesses confirm that their apps are in good working condition to avoid backlogs affecting user experience. Developers hire testers to push all possible links and buttons to ensure things work before they publish their software. Leading websites that pay app testers include UserCrowd, Userlytics, UTest, and Enroll.

Podcasting

Like blogging, podcasting has become a regular feature in online content, growing more popular by the day. With just a decent USB microphone sold for less than $100, you can start podcasting for free on platforms like Audacity.

Entertain People at Parties

Party entertainers do anything from magic to dressing in costume or performing at children's birthday parties. Your skill as a disc jockey or musical performer might spiral into a large source of income if you hone them well.

Become a Transcriber

A transcriptionist receives and types out audio files they receive from clients. These files could include videos, audio notes, phone calls, or legal documents. Websites like Rev, TranscribeMe, and Upwork often have paid transcription opportunities.

Three Things to Note Before Choosing a Side Hustle

While side hustles don't always grow into full-time jobs, many side hustlers eventually gravitate toward this option once their venture becomes profitable enough. Here are a few things to note before choosing a side hustle – especially one that might eventually become your career.

1.   Does the Idea Match Your Skills and Interests?

You want to choose a side hustle that closely matches your skills and interests to increase your chances of succeeding. Suppose you love photography; making money selling photos might be the way to go. Do you love pets? Maybe being a dog walker would be a great idea.

It'll also help to create a list of your skills and look for intersection points. If you're excellent at using photo editing software and like graphic design, maybe a freelance design role might suit you.

2.   Does the Idea Fit into Your Current Schedule?

If you already have an engagement that takes 40 hours of weekdays, committing too much time to a side hustle can lead to burnout. However, if you choose a side hustle related to your interests or passion, you might develop enough enthusiasm to maintain your part-time gigs.

3. Create a Strong Business Plan

Once you figure out the right side hustle that fits your interests and passions, it's time to create a business plan. The right business plan should concentrate on details that can help your hustle succeed.

Identify the right type of customer you want to target, how you'll find them, and build your business. It'll also help to familiarize yourself with the competition. Look out for others in similar businesses and check out what they charge or how they operate.

Finally, you want to decide how much money, if any, you'll need to create your business. What gadgets or tools do you already have? What licenses do you need to launch your brand? Answering these questions would guide you in creating a strong business plan to guide your side hustle or part-time business.

Exploring Entrepreneurial Finance and Funding Options

If you already have a business plan or idea, the next thing that'd likely come to your mind is accessing funding. Now, depending on the amount of capital you need, securing funding might be extremely straightforward or challenging.

However, a family or friend might provide their lobby for your new kitchen, but you'll definitely need substantial capital as your business outgrows that lobby and needs to be in a vantage position in town. The fact is, somewhere along the line in your business endeavor, you'll require some capital that could be way ahead of your current means.

Fortunately, many funding sources are available for early-stage entrepreneurs – apart from family, friends, or acquaintances. Here are some options that can provide you with ample inspiration for your next funding round.

Crowdfunding

Crowdfunding is raising money from a large group of investors, usually via an online platform. Entrepreneurs offer investment opportunities on one end of the platform, while a large group of people invest small amounts each toward meeting the entrepreneur's financial needs.

Startups would create compelling marketing content, outlining their business ideas, products, or projects in a crowdfunding campaign. On the other hand, investors contribute funds to convincing platforms in exchange for rewards, equity, or the fulfillment that comes from financing a promising venture.

Beyond providing entrepreneurs with the required funding, crowdfunding helps startups gain the needed exposure, validation, and helpful market feedback from potential clients and early adopters.

Bootstrapping

In bootstrapping, rather than rely on external funding sources, entrepreneurs utilize their own personal savings, business revenue, or loans from friends and family to finance their company's operations or expansion. It allows you to retain full control and ownership of your business. That way, you can rest assured of the total turnover in the event of a future sale.

Besides helping founders become more resourceful, bootstrapping instills discipline in you, compelling you to be more creative, efficient, and focused on generating revenue in the business's early stages. The path bootstrapping offers entrepreneurs might provide slower growth compared to ventures with external funding, but it also maximizes your possible rewards when it's time to sell your company.

SBA (Small Business Administration) Loans

If you live in the US, the US Small Business Administration provides small businesses with capital to finance their idea. These loans often apply to entrepreneurs who had challenges accessing finance through other means.

Besides offering lower interest rates, SBA loans also potentially offer longer repayment periods compared to other sources of entrepreneurial finance. The SBA guarantees a portion of the loan, reducing the risk for lenders who eventually provide the funding and raising startups' chances of securing approval.

Meanwhile, SBA loans also require personal guarantees from entrepreneurs. These guarantees mean the business owner or owners become personally liable for the loan. That also puts the entrepreneur's personal assets at risk should a loan default.

Grants

Grants are unlike loans or equity financing. Instead, grant providers provide non-refundable funds to startup founders, often with fewer restrictions. That gives entrepreneurs more flexibility in how they spend their funds.

Grants can improve your cash flow, attract other investors, and help to validate startups keen on achieving various social or environmental goals. That said, securing grants can be competitive as grant providers have to sift through thousands of proposals to award winners.

It'll help to conduct thorough research and align with all criteria contained in the grant's requirements. While grants are great income sources, I recommend you combine them with other financing options to maximize your business' success potential.

Long-Term Financial Planning

Short- and long-term goals are necessary to make your business or organization successful. Startups concentrating only on short-term goals overcome immediate challenges but fail to prevent them from recurring. Conversely, organizations that concentrate only on long-term goals may not live long enough to realize them.

It would help to find a balance between both short-term and long-term attitudes to financial planning.

Short-term goals include securing funding, reaching revenue targets, choosing the ideal business structure, and resolving cash flow issues. As you might have already noticed, most of the earlier sections in this chapter have already addressed short-term financial planning.

However, after establishing your short-term financial plans, creating a five- or ten-year plan is vital to help your company realize its ultimate goals. You want to ask questions like, 'Where will my brand be in a decade?' 'What do I want this brand to be remembered for, even if I sell it much later?'

Planning for the Long Haul

Both short-term and long-term financial plans are two sides of a coin. Whether it's a career in finance, an NGO, or a business idea, you can't plan for lifelong success without considering your current requirements. Sadly, a 2018 survey shows that 63% of small business owners only plan their next year in business.

Understandably, it can be challenging to turn aside from your daily tasks to concentrate on the future, but taking time aside to create a long-term strategy is one of the best ways to realize your long-term goals. Once you create your three- five- or ten-year plans, you can develop a short-term yearly plan to culminate right into your long-term goals.

But how do you plan your career or business idea for the long haul?

1. Define Your Mission

The first step to creating a strategic plan begins with creating a clear mission for your business. Write down one or two statements that show where you're headed. Be brief and realistic without being afraid of ambition.

Suppose you ran a barber's shop named Tim's Courts. Your mission might look something like, 'Tim's Court offers high-quality, affordable, and professional hair-care services to high-end clients in the Irvine Area.'

2. Set Long-Term Goals for Your Business

Mostly financially focused, these goals can help you achieve your overall mission.

Begin with your big picture, writing down the ideal future you plan for your business while ensuring it relates to your mission. Afterward, leverage our lesson on SMART goals to create specific, measurable, attainable, relevant, and time-bound goals for your brand.

So, let's revert to our example with Tim's Court. Tim has four long-term goals for his shop.

1. To become the No. 1 male hair stylist, dollar volume, in Irvine

2. Secure five-star annual ratings from every customer

3. Grow revenue to $5 million annually in the next three years.

4. Generate $500,000 annually in net income over the next three years.

3. Identify Broad Key Strategies

After delineating your goals, it'd help to outline the strategies you need to achieve them. They could range from building your facilities, purchasing equipment, or securing enough financing to realize your plans.

Tim's key strategies could include hiring and training top hair stylists and building a strong recognizable brand in his region. This could also mean that Tim would visit hair styling schools or attend recruiting events to get the best hands available for his business.

4. Measure Your Results

You always want to measure your progress as you execute the key strategies in your business plan. Select practical benchmarks that help you measure their performance consistently.

Finally, remember to be flexible on your business plan. Where one strategy doesn't perform well, consider changing it so you can still achieve your goals.

Workbook 5

Go on a no-spend challenge for a week. Write items you consider necessary and buy nothing else.

See if you can challenge your friends or siblings to join you in the challenge to see who'll save the most or break the challenge on day two!

Takeaway 5

Congratulations if you've read through the amazing funding opportunities for startup founders in this guide!

You've learned to:

- Budget intelligently

- Avoid bad debts

- Invest for the long haul

- Identify various side-hustling opportunities

- Explore various forms of entrepreneurial finance

- Plan for the long-haul

While there are many financing options, it can help to seek the guidance of experienced growth capital advisors or connect with other startup founders who have successfully funded their ideas. Aligning with knowledgeable advisors helps you tap into their wisdom and better understand the funding horizon enough to make informed choices and strategies to fuel your company's growth.

Chapter 6

Thriving in Remote Work Environments

"'Think about it this way: if you can create a three-hour chunk of non-distracted work time in your house, you will be more productive than the average office worker."
– Sharon Koifman

Succeeding in Virtual Workspaces

This chapter focuses on helping teens explore technology-driven opportunities to master time management, communication, and collaboration skills for success in virtual workspaces

Adapting in a Changing World

The world is speeding up, and a radical shift in our everyday lives and work culture directly results from modern-day technological advancements. How prepared are you to survive in a dynamic 21st-century environment where unending new technologies are poised to change how we network and do business?

Of course, skill sets that sold high during the Industrial Revolution will likely plummet in value, while new skills – like those I'll show you in this chapter – will take center stage.

The question is, how ready are you to adapt to a changing world where the required skill-sets may change every 10 years or less?

Entrepreneurs and businesses clinging to the past shoot themselves in the leg. Sticking to rigid and Roman-age hierarchical systems will fail to thrive in today's business environment. Traditional and outdated methods seek to control rather than inspire your team toward innovation and creativity.

Understandably, it can be challenging to adapt. Even nature is often adaptation-averse. However, as Charles Darwin's theory of evolution teaches, adaptation is necessary for any organization's survival.

If businesses don't adapt, they're bound to fail.

Fortunately, adaptability is a skill that can be learned. Here are a few ways to build it.

1. Learning to 'Play Again'

Your childhood isn't far behind you. And if there's anything not to leave behind as you grow into adulthood and your dream career, it's a child's resilience. Like you did as a child, leverage your imagination to view problems from different angles. Thinking creatively can easily present your mind with many new opportunities.

2. Visit Interesting Sites

Of course, you don't have to travel to the Bahamas or Marrakech to enjoy or have fun. There's nothing wrong with exploring a part of your city or town that you're unfamiliar with. It could be a restaurant you haven't tried or a popular fall you only saw on the TV. Little explorations like this help to tinker with your adventurous and adaptable traits.

3. Don't Hold a Negative Fear of Getting Left Behind

Rather than have a negative fear of falling behind, how about turning that dread into a motivation to keep moving? Admit that the world will always change, and be comfortable with that discovery. Rather than have it cripple you, let it spur you into action.

4. Never Stop Reading

Reading is great for several reasons. First, it helps you learn new skills and obtain knowledge. Second, it also helps to keep your brain malleable and alive.

5. Experiment Occasionally

Try a new food, design something small. Experimenting and trying out new things often require a degree of critical thinking and problem-solving skills that can come in handy during work hours.

6. When in a Team, Communicate Changes Early

Are you leading a team that needs to adapt to new technological changes? It'll help to explain the 'why' behind your team's transitions using various helpful tools. Town hall meetings, video conferences, and team-wide emails are great options.

In the remaining part of this chapter, I'll show you various technologically-driven opportunities in the remote work revolution. You'll also find how to master your time to boost productivity while 'working from anywhere', communicate effectively with your team, navigate online tools, showcase your remote work skills to employers, and have fun while at it all.

Technology-Driven Opportunities

Business leaders know that one way their organizations can drive innovation and improve their products and services is by taking advantage of technology. As new and advanced technologies get on the scene, businesses can leverage new tools to streamline their processes, create new opportunities, and boost their overall customer experience.

However, somewhere at the center of leveraging technology for business growth is every company's tech staff. Technical staff members are often the brains behind everything from cloud technologies to SaaS tools, website interfaces, and advanced security systems.

In a Future of Jobs Report 2023, the World Economic Forum predicts that technology adoption will remain a key driver of business transformation over the next five years. According to another research by German researchers in the Leipzig Graduate School of Management, tech-driven entrepreneurship activities will always lead to innovation in small and medium businesses.

That suggests to you, dear reader, that pursuing tech-driven opportunities places you in one of the most promising career paths today.

Here are some of the top 10 tech-driven opportunities of the future.

1. AI and Machine Learning Specialists

As AI and machine learning technologies dominate work environments, there's an increasing demand for experts in this field. As a result, the demand for experts who can design, develop, and implement AI and machine learning technology is expected to increase.

2. Data Science and Analysis

The data revolution has overtaken the world – companies are learning to leverage data from various sources to analyze their market and inform crucial decisions.

3. Robotics Engineering

You've probably heard of a restaurant served by robots mostly – or a hotel whose waiters and 'room service professionals' are literally machines. But robotics and automation technology are going beyond the hospitality sectors to delicate sectors like healthcare! Businesses need engineers and technicians to design, program, and maintain these robotic systems.

4. Blockchain Development

As blockchain technology and cryptocurrency increase in application, so does the need for blockchain technology. Meanwhile, blockchain technology keeps breaking new grounds beyond cryptocurrency. This development, among many other things, means that skilled developers with expertise in blockchain will be in demand.

5. E-Commerce and Digital Marketing Specialists

With the growth of online retail and digital marketing over conventional marketing strategies, the demand for experts in this field is bound to increase. Specialists in this field range from social media marketing experts to online advertising pros to e-commerce marketing specialists.

6. Medical Technology

The medical industry is always in demand – and so are medical technologies. Fortunately, medical technology keeps advancing, giving rise to new healthcare jobs for which a significantly smaller section of the population is qualified.

7. Remote Work Facilitators

As remote work becomes more popular, the demand for professionals facilitating remote collaboration will increase. These professionals will help to enhance team communication toward maximizing the team's productivity.

8. Virtual Reality (VR) and Augmented Reality (AR) Developers

Perhaps no other decade has seen a burst of VR and AR products as the last decade. As AR and VR technologies evolve and find applications in various industries like healthcare, gaming, entertainment, and education, the potential demand for skilled developers is bound to remain on the rise.

9. Sustainable and Renewable Energy Experts

There's an increasing focus on environmental sustainability and renewable energy in the 21st century. And this emphasis is expected to grow in the next decade. Expectedly, as the emphasis on sustainable processes increases, the rise in career opportunities related to the fields of renewable energy, green technology, and environmental conservation is inevitable.

10. Cybersecurity Specialists

While the world keeps celebrating the benefits of technology and innovation, we also have to catch up with the downsides that threaten advancements in civilization. Technology is advancing, and so is tech-based fraud. Cybersecurity experts help businesses protect sensitive systems and data from increasingly costly cyber threats.

Remote Work Revolution

Many organizations shifted to remote during the COVID-19 pandemic and have not left the arena since. After the pandemic waned and social distancing regulations eased, employees showed reluctance to return to rigid work settings. In fact, a report from Cardiff and Southampton universities showed that 88% of remote workers wished to continue to work from home to some extent post-pandemic.

Various Fortune 500 companies have embraced the remote work revolution over the last few years. For instance, Jack Dorsey, Twitter's CEO, told employees in 2020 that they could work from home forever if they so desired.

Meta (then Facebook) also allowed its employees to work from home – amplifying the reality of the remote work revolution. Nationwide Insurance, another Fortune 500 company, has chosen to close its small corporate offices and relocate its over 30,000 employees to remote positions or one of its other branches.

Why Remote Work is Important

Remote work empowers employees with emerging tech solutions that help to enhance their productivity. According to a report, over 50% of employers say the main benefit of remote work is increased productivity. With that said, here are other reasons why remote work is important to employees and their organizations.

1. An Outcome-Based Rather than a Time-Based Focus

Remote work concentrates on better project outcomes rather than time spent at work. This approach encourages teammates to improve communication and collaborate among themselves. It also encourages teams to concentrate more on goals and project offerings rather than office politics, bureaucracy, and other activities that don't directly impact their teams' key goals and client needs.

2. Promises a Happier and More Balanced Workforce

According to a report from Amerisleep, 80% of remote workers said they feel less stressed when working from home. That's because remote work removes commute time and enhances flexibility, which can help teams achieve more in a day than they would if they spent all work time in an office.

Additionally, remote work ensures you can eat lunch with family, walk with your pets, and enjoy more freedom with your work schedule.

3. Saves Costs

Working remotely saves you various costs involved in working in walk-in offices. Businesses in physical locations often spend on various expenses like rent, office maintenance, employee commuting, daily lunches, and more. That way, employees can use their human and material resources more efficiently to gain better results.

These advantages are exciting motivations to consider choosing a career in remote work.

Understanding a Remote Work Agreement

A remote work agreement is a deal between remote workers and their employer that defines the employees' commitments and responsibilities. Your employer may draw up this contract at the beginning of your employment journey (in the job description that advertised the role) or after you onboard the organization.

The typical remote work contract includes sections like:

- Work arrangements

- Compensation and benefits

- Requirements, provisions, and arrangements for computer equipment and software

- Provisions and arrangements for telephone and internet connectivity

- Travel and other expense reimbursements

Your remote contract may or may not include any of these sections. But these five are major sections of many remote work contracts.

At other times, remote work contacts may include sections on taxes, data security, supplies, insurance, safety, liabilities, and dependent care.

Mastering Time Management and Productivity

If productivity is the focus of remote work, then mastering time management skills has to be one of the most relevant skills for a successful career in remote work.

According to a report by Starling Bank, microbusinesses (companies with less than 10 employees) spend 15 hours weekly on administrative roles. Meanwhile, solopreneurs (people who run businesses 'single-handedly') spend 31% of their weekly time sorting finances.

Now, spending so much time on administrative tasks and financial housekeeping is a less-than-efficient use of time.

Time management involves planning how to efficiently use and deliberately control how much time you spend toward maximizing productivity. Let's get right onto my productivity hacks to get more done in less time while working from home.

1. Create Realistic Timelines

I've been there, and many people are too. Remote workers tend to overestimate their capacity to get things done. Scientists call this tendency the 'planning fallacy.' Avoid setting overly optimistic delivery estimates. Add time buffers in-between tasks so that the overall schedule stays in place even when one task takes longer than usual.

2. Prioritize with To-Do Lists

To-do lists can be extremely efficient productivity hacks. However, if you don't exercise enough care, your list can get so large that you don't know what to do first or next.

One tool that helps people prioritize effectively is called the Eisenhower Matrix. This decision matrix helps you break down your list into sections such as:

- **Do immediately:** for tasks with defined deadlines or those you've put off for so long that are now overdue

- **Schedule for later:** for important tasks with no defined deadline

- **Delegate:** tasks someone else can do

- **Delete:** tasks you can eliminate because they're not critical to your mission or goals

3. Tackle the Most Difficult Tasks First

Anyone could face distractions. And it could be a few minutes of a phone call, a notification from your social media app, a favor from a colleague, or that pile of dirty clothes long overdue for the cleaners.

As Brian Tracy recommends in his anti-productivity best-seller *Eat That Frog,* the best way to overcome procrastination is to tackle the most important or largest task first. You want to tackle the tasks you're likely to put off for later.

Those 'dreary' tasks are what Brian Tracy calls the frog. Once you've eaten the frog, it's time to move on to other tasks.

4. Avoid Multitasking

Multitasking helps you cut efficiency and can even be lethal to your health. According to a report from the American Psychological Association, multitasking involves 'switching costs' that slash productivity. Switching between tasks might cost only a few seconds for each switch. However, it adds up if you multitask frequently, wastes more time, and increases your chances of making mistakes.

5. Learn to Say No

You have only so much energy in a day. And your energy would likely wane as time ticks. One way to avoid half-baked work is to understand your limits and know when to say no. It'll help to recognize your strengths and weaknesses. Concentrate on your strengths, and, if possible, delegate what others can do better or faster.

6. Maintain a Clean 'Work Desk'

National Geographic reports that neuroscience and psychology link the effects of clutter on mental health and cognition. That implies, among many other things, that visual clutter can increase people's stress and anxiety levels while you're repeatedly triggering fight-or-flight response.

It'll help to toss away any papers you can shred or recycle. Also clear out any nonessentials and place daily tools within easy reach. Meanwhile, your 'work desk' extends to your computer files and shared drives. Organize your files to help you and your team members easily identify them.

7. Use Time Management Tools

Besides the Eisenhower Matrix, it'll help to leverage other time management and productivity apps to boost your work productivity. Some other helpful automation software includes Slack, Dropbox, Google Calendar, and Lucidchart.

Effective Communication in Virtual Settings

Three out of every five employees work remotely. And that number promises to grow. But that doesn't mean many teams and organizations finally understand the nuances of coordinating teams working from different locations.

For instance, virtual work procedures could lead to highly misunderstood, unclear, or ineffective communications that can impair a client-business relationship. While a positive in-person work environment in an office is beneficial, communicating effectively can help you translate a similar culture online.

Rather than relapse into walk-in coffee discussions or in-person work environments, managers can leverage effective communication to encourage their team and clearly communicate their expectations.

Managers aren't the only professionals who need to understand effective communication.

Employees in virtual work settings also need to communicate effectively with colleagues and superiors to build efficient workflows, collaboration, and the team's overall staff morale.

If you choose a career in remote work, here are helpful tips to communicate effectively in a virtual work setting.

1. Provide Adequate Feedback

From emails to video chats, screenshots and more, there are plenty of tools to help you provide valuable feedback to your team members. But communicating feedback goes beyond sending information back-and-forth.

It'll help to ensure your recipients receive your information correctly. Wrong information could be worse than no information at all.

Mind you, be honest and empathetic when providing feedback, suggestions, or corrections on work done. Discuss with the team what they're doing rightly, what needs improvement, or what they're doing poorly.

Let your team members know you value their recommendations or questions. That way, they're more likely to avoid 'holding back' to protect your feelings.

2. Ensure Information Accessibility

Keep your colleagues or supervisors informed about every major or minor development. Inform them about any project due dates or changes in milestones.

The more you share information about the workload and current project status, the more chances other team members will hold themselves accountable.

Lastly, you can also convert some of the time spent reaching out to team members into a chance to reach out to them and see how they're faring. That way, you'd foster trust between your team members and increase your chances of receiving assistance or helpful feedback.

3. Implement a Review System

One way to ensure employees are on track to achieving their objectives is having a clear and thorough review system. This review system could include anything from a weekly review meeting to a monthly reward system that grades all employees' performances.

Meanwhile, these virtual meetings can also serve as an avenue for answering questions, setting new goals, and providing constructive feedback.

4. Bond with Your Team

Building a team goes beyond putting together individuals to work on a project. Instead, it's about creating a bond that simplifies communication between them.

The more managers understand the remote team, the more they can communicate and empathize with other team members. Similarly, the more employees understand their managers and other employees, the more they can empathize and communicate effectively while being vulnerable and honest.

I'm sure you get the drift.

How about proposing a virtual lunch or other fun activities to break up busy patterns? How about holding in-person meetings or attending conferences together to relieve the routine of remote working and 'catch up' differently?

5. Create Knowledge Repositories

Centralized knowledge repositories can come in handy in various ways. One, it ensures everyone is on the same page by making information easily accessible to all. These repositories can also allow team members to reuse and adjust ideas as processes and systems evolve.

New members can also utilize these knowledge spaces to access all technical and procedural information when joining the team. That way, you can rest assured you aren't missing anything important when briefing new entries.

Navigating Online Collaboration Tools

Online collaboration helps employees and their supervisors perform various tasks, share and access resources, discuss, perform online activities, and do many more. Popular examples are Skype, Trello, Slack, and Google Docs.

According to a report, in-person meetings will account for only one-quarter of team conversations by 2024. In another report, the global market size of the collaboration software market could reach $40.78 billion by 2028.

These figures (and more) suggest that remote and hybrid work environments require a stack of online collaborative tools to boost their productivity and make them less dependent on in-person offices.

Here are five leading collaboration tools you need to learn – even before you might 'need' them to work on a remote team or workplace.

1. Google Docs

Google Docs is an efficient word processing and collaboration tool that lets users create, edit, and share documents, spreadsheets, and presentations on the go. With similar features to the Microsoft Word software, Docs lets you insert images, format your texts, and insert links.

It's accessible to multiple users at the same time. Users can also leave comments on specific sections of the documents. Meanwhile, Docs also integrates with other collaboration tools like Google Sheets and Google Drive.

2. Trello

Trello is a popular project management tool that lets individuals and teams organize their tasks, projects, and to-do lists intuitively and visually. Trello lets users create boards demonstrating projects or goals, with lists and cards they can move around as priorities change.

Trello also offers helpful features like comments, checklists, and attachments to enhance effective communication among team members.

3. Slack

Slack is a cloud-based communication tool that lets you intuitively communicate and collaborate with other team members. The easy-to-use collaboration app lets users create channels (or dedicated spaces for specific topics or projects).

Slack also integrates with other online collaboration tools like Zoom, Trello, and Google Drive.

4. Zoom

The popular video conferencing app has a simple interface with intuitive controls almost anyone can understand. Zoom is an excellent tool for video-based virtual meetings, with high-quality video and audio features that can hold up to 1,000 participants.

Zoom also lets users share their screens during presentations, demonstrations, or other collaborative work. Users can also record meetings or webinars for subsequent sharing with others.

5. Dropbox

Dropbox is a file-hosting platform that lets you store and share files and folders with others. With over 700 million registered users, the cloud-based collaboration tool is definitely one of the most popular tools in its industry or field.

Dropbox has definitely revolutionized how we store and share information. Other Dropbox features include automatic backup and file syncing. Dropbox is compatible with multiple devices and operating systems, such as Mac, iOS, Android, Linux, and Windows.

Showcasing Remote Work Skills to Employers

The ability to work remotely without the close, in-person supervision of office routines is a skill in itself. Showing employers a track record of successful remote work experiences helps increase your chances of getting more work-from-home opportunities.

However, while you may not have held a remote work role before, it doesn't mean you can't succeed as a remote employee. You want to know what skills remote team managers want in an employee and how to show them in your resume.

These tips demonstrate remote work skills in your resume, whether or not you have proper remote work experience.

What Skills Do Remote Work Managers Want in an Employee?

Not every hiring manager for a remote role insists their candidates must have remote work experience. However, they want to see that you are self-motivated and can work independently.

However, if you have some experience working remotely, it's an excellent idea to highlight this experience in your resume; it might give you a soft landing. A potential employer would likely get attracted to your remote work experience as it shows you possess skills like:

- Communication

- Collaboration

- Collaboration

- Time and Task management

All these skills are paramount in remote teams.

Employers also want to see what you've potentially achieved while working remotely. For instance, they may want to know if you worked with a remote team or were the sole remote employee in the previous role.

Showcasing Your Remote Work Experience in Your Resume

A summary of your qualifications is usually at the top of your resume and is the first thing hiring managers will see. Your qualification summary, which provides a brief overview of your professional experience, can make an excellent spot to show you have remote work experience.

For instance, if you're seeking a remote administrative role, your summary could include something like:

- Over 3 years of administrative assistantship experience

- 2 years' experience working from home 100% of the time

- Expertise in scheduling and collaboration tools, memo drafting, and report writing

- Successfully planned over 100+ on-site and off-site meetings

Placing your remote work experience in the summary section will help the recruiter see instantly that you have the requisite experience working independently from home.

Another way to demonstrate your remote work experience is by including it in the location section. Here are three ways to do this:

- List the organization's corporate location when using the city/state format. However, indicate you performed the work remotely in the first sentence or bullet point.

- Indicate 'remote work' instead of your past office's city/state

- Include it in your work descriptions, deliberately detailing how you performed off-site.

- Showcase skills you built while working remotely, such as being a self-starter, an excellent communicator, or an outstanding manager.

Otherwise, create a new section that reads 'remote work experience' to list companies where you worked remotely. You only want to be sure you aren't distracting the application reviewer from your best qualifications by inadvertently pushing other relevant non-remote experience lower in the resume.

What If I Don't Have a Remote Work Experience?

If you haven't held a remote position before, it'll help to brainstorm times you worked at home. Look at a remote experience from a different lens than an employer.

You want to ask yourself questions like, 'Do I often work from home?' 'Do I regularly bring work home to complete outside regular office hours?'

Even if you haven't worked at home before, you've likely worked with co-workers and clients who lived elsewhere. Bring up those experiences with them and convert them into sharable remote skills.

Have you ever had to coordinate live meetings across multiple time zones? How do you manage a crisis that develops on a project with team members scattered in various locations?

Highlight your success in these areas while showing how you accomplished your goals and solved the problems. Take some time to dig deep and ruminate over what you do and how you do it. Doing so can demonstrate that you have all the skills to be a great remote employee.

Industry Trends and Forecast

While this chapter explains how to adapt to a changing world, it'll do great also to include how to understand when a market is changing or where it is headed.

When companies, team leaders, or entrepreneurs fail to make accurate forecasts, it could lead them to fatal errors.

As new technologies, emerging finance, and other socio-cultural or economic revolutions come into the scene, you'll need to decide what trend looks promising and which is most likely a fluke. And to achieve that, you'll always want to have a holistic ('all-rounder') approach that shows you every side of the die.

But you might be asking, 'How do I gather enough well-rounded, unbiased information to predict the future of trends to stay relevant in your industry as an entrepreneur, leader, professional, or employee?'

Your answer is one word – Information.

Gather as much information as you can to determine the leading factors behind the trends or news everyone hears in the news. While newspapers and magazines are excellent sources of trends and forecasts, let's see other helpful sources with vital information for both large and small industries.

- **Statista**

Statista includes statistics and studies from market research institutions, business organizations, scientific publications, government agencies, and more. Statista covers various fields from business to media, technology, society, education, and more from scores of countries.

- **Sage Data, powered by Data Planet**

Formerly Data-Planet Statistical Datasets, Sage Data includes over 52 billion data points in over 6.2 billion datasets sourced from over 70 public and private data providers. Sage Data also lets users manipulate datasets and compare multiple indicators and sources while charting trends against time and spatially representing data without additional software programs.

The platform includes information from data providers like Zillow, US Stock

Market Prices, Factset Corporate Fundamentals, and choice international market indices and exchanges.

- **EIU Online**

EIU Online includes publications from the Economist Intelligence Unit (EIU) that analyze and forecast the economic, political, and business climates of over 200 nations. Current EIU reports include Country Finance, Country Commerce, Country Reports, Global Forecasting Service, and Premium Country Access for China.

- **Nexis Uni**

Nexis Uni features over 15,000 news, business, and legal sources from LexisNexis. The user-friendly platform also includes U.S. Supreme Court decisions dating back to 1790. Users can quickly discover all types of content and enjoy personalization features like alerts, annotated documents, and saved searches in collaborative workspaces.

Workbook 6

List a new collaboration tool every week over a one-month period. If possible, share your findings with friends and possibly introduce these tools to your friends or colleagues in various teams.

Takeaway 6

The job market is changing rapidly, as we've seen in the last two decades. New technologies and societal shifts are leading to the emergence of new careers. As a budding professional or teen, one way to stay relevant in the coming age is to develop adaptable skills like critical thinking, problem-solving, creativity, and a willingness to embrace lifelong learning.

Even if you truly haven't worked with anyone outside an office, it doesn't mean you don't have the necessary skills to be a successful remote employee. Work-from-home roles require candidates to have strong communication skills, organizational skills, computer skills, and the ability to work independently and avoid distractions.

Chapter 7

Entrepreneurship: Carving Your Path

'Dream big. Start small. But most of all, start'
–Simon Sinek

Cultivating an Entrepreneurial Mindset

Developing an Entrepreneurial Mindset

It doesn't have to take a long time for you to develop an entrepreneurial mindset – as long as you don't get lost in the 'rut' many young teens find themselves across America.

'What's the rut?' you're probably asking.

It's the 'get good grades, fall into line, and get a good job' line – yeah, you've probably heard that more than you've heard many other motivational lines already.

Schoolteachers often get so concerned about you getting good jobs that they might hardly mention to you that you could start – and successfully run – your own business.

But this book can relieve them of that burden – at least for you.

Right?

How about we check out one high-school teen who refused to accept the get-good-grade-and-get-a-good-job stereotype and worked his way to becoming one of the youngest billionaires in the world today?

His name is Ryan Breslow.

Born and raised in North Miami Beach, Florida, Ryan Breslow taught himself to code in middle school via online tutorials and YouTube videos. Beyond discovering a passion for coding, Ryan discovered and developed his entrepreneurial mindset by participating in various business challenge contests and activities while still in high school.

Leveraging his coding and business skills while in high school, Ryan started and operated several businesses while also helping businesses set up e-commerce sites. Ryan's academic merits, social consciousness, and business acumen paid off – he got a scholarship to Stanford University to study computer science.

But Ryan would soon have his share of entrepreneurial fever. Only two years into Stanford, Ryan dropped out of school and founded Bolt, a payment processing firm worth around $5 billion, according to Forbes estimate.

Meanwhile, Ryan Breslow also runs an early-stage wellness startup, Love, which he founded in 2022.

Now, Ryan didn't just learn to try his hands on business ideas he got while in his teens; he *developed* and honed the right MINDSET from small attempts to help him build a billion-dollar company.

Well, What Is an Entrepreneurial Mindset?

An entrepreneurial mindset includes a set of beliefs, thought processes, and worldviews that drive entrepreneurial behavior. The average startup founder believes they can improve their situation and live the way they want. They also believe in their ability to learn, grow, adapt, and succeed.

While conventional workers seek to increase their income by brushing up their resumes for better-paid jobs, entrepreneurs think of growing or starting a business to grow their income.

Now, here's the good news. Anyone can develop an entrepreneurial mindset, including you.

That reminds me of a famous quote by Henry Ford, 'whether you think you can or think you can't – you're right.'

How Entrepreneurs Think

Do you want to learn how to grow an entrepreneurial mindset? Check out these ten common characteristics that show how entrepreneurs think.

1. Independent

Entrepreneurs hardly follow the crowd or look to others to receive instructions. Instead, they look inward to carve out a unique path for themselves.

2. Responsible

Successful entrepreneurs are independent because they take full responsibility. Entrepreneurs don't blame others for their life situation. Instead, they empower themselves by taking responsibility to improve their lives.

It doesn't matter whether they're failing or succeeding in life. Even when they weren't directly responsible for a fault, successful entrepreneurs take responsibility for it.

3. Abundant

Perhaps few quotes tell the story of an entrepreneur than this from Robert Kiyosaki, author of *Rich Dad, Poor Dad*:

'I have never met a rich person who has never lost any money. But I have met a lot of poor people who have never lost a dime.

Successful entrepreneurs don't hoard money or knowledge. Instead, they're generous, open, and have a you-get-what-you-give mindset.'

4. Goal-oriented

High-achieving entrepreneurs don't have wishes or dreams – they have goals and plans they're constantly pursuing. Successful entrepreneurs create specific, measurable, attainable, relevant, and time-sensitive goals.

5. Not afraid to fail

Entrepreneurs look at failure differently than most people. Successful businessmen don't fear failure – rather, they appreciate it, considering each failure as a stepping stone to learn from, helping them move closer to success.

Failing never means you're a failure, just that something didn't work how you wanted. And you've got to try again if you still cherish your initial goals.

6. Learning-oriented

Entrepreneurs are growth-oriented. They believe they can grow, learn new things, and develop new skills. They also believe that, with consistent effort, they can shape themselves into whoever they want to be.

7. Feedback-seeking

The most successful entrepreneurs learn from others' feedback to speed up their growth process. Rather than seeking validation, entrepreneurs seek ways to improve via feedback and other reflective activities.

8. Action-oriented

Entrepreneurs understand that knowledge without action is meaningless. Unlike 'wantrepreneurs' who read books, watch videos, and plan without actually getting down to *work*, entrepreneurs create and follow a basis for action.

9. Self-accepting

Successful entrepreneurs accept themselves as they are. Rather than focus on who they are, successful business owners work on becoming the person they want to be.

10. Problem-Solving

Entrepreneurs develop critical thinking skills that enable them to solve problems. And this should be the center of every business anyway. Netflix cures boredom, Uber gets you to your destination, and restaurants help you avoid hunger. Entrepreneurs understand this and work to create solutions to problems around them.

Identifying Business Opportunities and Ideas

Perhaps another top aspect of entrepreneurial thinking is the keen ability to identify business opportunities and ideas.

While anyone can think of a new idea for a business, successful entrepreneurs can tell if the idea is a business opportunity.

A great business opportunity either fulfills market demand, solves customer pain points, or improves an existing product.

Do you already have a set of business ideas and need to determine their viability? Or are you considering starting up your business? Regardless of your current situation, you want to familiarize yourself with different business opportunities and learn to identify them.

Let's see three types of business opportunities to search for, how to identify them, and maintain a pliable mindset for an entrepreneurial mindset.

Types of Entrepreneurship Opportunities to Search For

1. Jobs that Need to be Done

Clayton Christensen, an American academic, devised what's called the jobs-to-be-done theory. The theory states that people don't purchase a product.

Instead, they 'hire' it to do a job.

Christensen explains this theory using research McDonald's executives made concerning milkshake sales – which sold the highest in the morning. Their research showed that customers hired milkshakes to keep them occupied and full during their morning commutes.

At its base, entrepreneurship involves using available resources to fill unmet needs in the market. It lets you lay hold of a reason – however flimsy – that causes customers to buy your product or service. Once you understand this reason, develop or improve on a product that seals this need perfectly, and your chances of succeeding in business will improve dramatically.

2. Low-End Market Opportunities

In a related theory, Christensen explains that the key to identifying market gaps is to understand what he calls the theory of disruptive innovation.

In the theory of disruptive innovation, Christensen shows how companies with fewer resources can break into existing markets and disrupt ongoing startups that own segments of them.

However, there are two types of disruptive innovation: low-end and new-market.

In low-end disruption, new businesses enter the market and claim the lowest market segment without threatening existing companies.

With time, the new entrant moves into higher market segments, technically pushing or motivating older companies to seek higher-profit enterprises. The cycle continues until the new entrant takes over the incumbent's market.

Choosing this method helps you avoid directly colluding or competing with existing businesses for top market segments. That way, you also increase your chances of succeeding in your business attempts.

3. New Market Opportunities

Here's the other type of disruptive innovation. New market opportunities provide ample opportunities to succeed as an entrepreneur.

Here's how they work. Suppose your business creates a new segment in an existing market – a new segment that's probably tired of current companies or increasingly exploited due to an existing company's monopoly.

Creating an opportunity that makes the product more appealing and less expensive while maintaining 'good enough' quality can help you create and capture a new market segment.

Once you've identified the problems you want to solve, conducted adequate market research, and queried the process, you're on your way to creating a product that can disrupt the market and carve a segment for your service or product.

Creating a Solid Business Plan

Without having a solid business plan, many investors won't even grant an entrepreneur an audience. Meanwhile, your business plan must be outstanding to win investment funds, grants, and even credit facilities.

A comprehensive, well-thought-out business plan is crucial to the success of corporate managers and entrepreneurs. Trust me; this is beyond the most challenging writing assignment you ever had.

You'll need a well-conceived and well-presented plan to win the necessary support and investment for your idea. Additionally, the right business plan must describe the company's project accurately and attractively.

The ideal business plan must detail your current status, current needs, and projected future. It should also include and justify financial projections, personal needs, and marketing decisions convincingly and logically.

Now, I'm sure I am not losing you already. In the following paragraphs, let's break down the steps to writing an effective business plan.

Writing an Effective Business Plan

1. **Begin with an Executive Summary:** Your business plan's first page has this page. Like an elevator pitch, your executive summary should include a mission statement, a brief description of your products or services, and a broad summary of your financial growth plans.

2. **Describe Your Company:** Your company description should contain information like your business' registered name (if you've registered it already), your location, and key people on your team (including their areas of expertise). Your company description should also cover your business history and structure (e.g., sole proprietorship, partnership, or corporation, etc.).

3. **Write Your Business Goals:** Spell out exactly what you want to accomplish in the short- and long-term. Here's where you can explain why you need the funds and how they can help your business grow. The key is clearly explaining your idea and HOW the investment will grow your company.

4. **Products or Services Description:** Share details here about the products or services you offer or intend to offer. Also include information on the pricing model, typical customers, supply chain, and sales and distribution strategy.

5. **Show Information from Your Market Research:** Lenders and investors want to know what separates you from your competition. Your market analysis section explains your competitors, what they do well, and what you can do better.

6. **Outline Your Marketing and Sales Plan:** Show how you intend to convince customers to purchase your goods or services. Also, tell how you intend to develop customer loyalty and retain your clients.

7. **Conduct a Business Financial Analysis:** This section might not be necessary if you're just starting your business. However, existing businesses will do well to include income or profit-and-loss statements, net profit margin, and other metrics that show the business' financial footing.

8. **Make Financial Projections:** Demonstrate how your business will generate enough profit to earn investors a decent return or repay the loan. You'll also provide your business' monthly or quarterly sales, expenses, and profit projections over at least three years.

9. **Add Other Information in an Appendix:** List any supporting documents or information you couldn't fit elsewhere. This could include resumes of key employees, licenses, or bank statements,

A caveat for creating an effective business plan: Provide accurate information as much as possible by carefully analyzing your past financial statements before providing projections. While your goals may be ambitious, you also want to ensure they're realistic enough.

Marketing and Branding for Young Entrepreneurs

Remember Ryan Breslow and his story?

Well, stats show there are more likely Ryan Breslow types today than ten years ago before the *original* Ryan discovered Bolt. A recent study shows that 60% of teens would start their businesses rather than work regular jobs.

Notably, entrepreneurship has become a popular career choice for many young folks – and I hope that includes you!

But it all begins with personal branding – which should come with little or no effort. People will connect your identity and certain things with you. Meanwhile, branding yourself or your business to a niche market can become a powerful tool to promote your identity and what you can offer the market.

The expected result is to open doors for better opportunities that drive consumers to your business.

With that said, here are helpful tips that can help you successfully brand yourself as an entrepreneur.

1. **Define Your Target Audience**: Who is your business trying to reach? What are specific needs you can fill for them?

2. **Create a Unique Selling Proposition (USP)**: What makes your business different from other entrepreneurs in your field?

3. **Develop a Strong Visual Identity**: Create an immediately recognizable logo and other graphic elements for your brand. Research shows that more than half of the first impressions of brands are visual.

4. **Be Consistent**: Consistency is key to the success of every brand. It'll help to remain consistent in your branding approach – except when you want to rebrand. For instance, use the same themes, colors, fonts, and overall aesthetic across your social media channels, websites, and materials.

5. **Share Your Story with the World**: What drives your entrepreneurship goals? Why did you become an entrepreneur? It'll help to share your story with potential clients and customers to help them connect with you on a personal level.

6. **Embrace Sustainability Early**: Sustainability includes everything from using less energy and water to marketing your business online rather than with print media. Sustainable business not only promises lower operating costs, it is also more appealing to customers who will thank you for contributing to a better and greener world.

7. **Build Relationships**: Build a personal relationship with your customers by learning more about them. For instance, depending on your industry, asking questions about their hobbies, music, or special days can help foster a long-term relationship with them. Also, attend or sponsor community events to promote your brand to new and local audiences.

8. **Track Your Progress**: Keeping track of your brand with metrics like website traffic and social media management can help you verify how effective your strategy is. It'll also help weed out or adjust poorly performing activities and divert resources toward more effective marketing tools.

9. **Leverage Social Media**: Social media can be a powerful tool to market your brand. Use social media to its fullest potential via hashtags, running ads, or creating engaging content.

10. **Hire A Professional**: Hire a professional if you aren't sure of where to begin your branding. A branding agency can help you develop a strong visual identity and create consistent content across all your marketing platforms.

Managing Finances and Cash Flow in a Startup

Cash is king for any business – and especially for startups. Managing cash will undoubtedly be a top priority to grow any successful business.

Meanwhile, what is cash flow in startups anyway?

Cashflow refers to the inflow and outflow of cash in your business. Your cash flow can be either negative or positive. A quick way to calculate cash flow is to subtract all outflows and payments from your total income.

Mind you, your cash flow report is different from a profit and loss account. Your cash flow includes non-cash items like depreciation, amortization, credit sales, and purchases.

A positive cash flow says you have more cash at the closing date than the starting date, while a negative cash flow shows you lack money to run your firm.

Every startup must regularly prepare cash-flow statements that help it keep track of how much money goes in and out of the organization.

Maintaining a positive cash flow is necessary for your business to thrive or survive and avoid liquidation. Here are expert tips to manage your start-up's finances and cash flow.

1. Prepare Your Cash flow Statement

Identify all sources of business income, revenue, and expenditure. You can have more than one income source. Make a mental note of these sources and record how much cash they generate. Remember, your existing and potential investors and stakeholders will need to occasionally see your business's cash flow to assess your business' performance.

2. Keep Personal and Business Funds Separate

Keep your business funds from private funds to avoid uncertainty in determining your business' performance. Doing this will also help you avoid errors when filing tax returns. Of course, you already know that mixing your personal and business funds will make calculating your cash flow more difficult.

3. Leverage Tax Relief and save Money

Many entrepreneurs sadly pay more tax than they should, often because they don't understand how to prepare their tax returns or aren't leveraging tax reliefs. Leverage tax reliefs to reduce your tax bills, or speak with a professional to guide you toward protecting your cash flow and improving your ROI.

4. Set Cash Flow Forecasts

Creating regular and accurate cash flow projections can help you identify prospective problems beforehand. Setting cash flow forecasts can also help companies make sound decisions based on their estimations or forecasts.

A good way to begin is by creating a list of assumptions, such as the price of raw materials, the projected selling price, or expected inflation over the next three years.

5. Prepare a Budget

Prepare a budget based on your income and expenditure – and stick to it. Look into your financial statements to see if you can cut any unnecessary expenses to save money. Meanwhile, remember that your budget isn't static and can change as market situations change.

6. Build an Emergency Cash Reserve

Create an emergency cash reserve to meet immediate needs when your regular bank account is in the red or inaccessible. Doing this protects you from spending your savings or getting into debt.

7. Encourage Fast Payments and Invoice Issuances

Avoid being too generous with your credit terms. Issue invoices immediately after a sale while providing seamless payment options for your clients.

Facilitate fast payments, either to or from your company. If your customers don't pay on time, consider creating a polite invoicing strategy or even take formal actions when necessary.

Doing this not only improves your cash flow stability and growth but also gives a positive impression to the brand about your integrity with both incoming and outgoing payments.

8. Use Accounting Software

There's no shying away from accounting tools and software in the tech era. Manual accounting processes won't fit. You want to look for relevant accounting software to help fulfill your business' daily requirements and manage cash flow. However, hiring a professional can also help if you need help in this area.

9. Regularly Check Your Business' Financial Health

All said and done, conduct a regular financial health check-up to measure and interpret your business's cash flow. Study your most recent profit and loss statements to understand how well you managed your cash in the previous month or quarter.

Remember, poor cash management is a leading reason for business failure, as companies can no longer fund liabilities and meet their goals.

Navigating Legalities

Legal regulations are always changing. That means understanding how to navigate legalities is vital to protecting your business' success. While achieving an entirely compliant business can be challenging, doing so brings benefits, including avoiding heavy legal, financial, or social consequences.

Follow on for essential advice to help you stay ahead of legal and regulatory changes, avoid potential dangers, and ensure your company stays on the path to success.

Choosing the Right Business Structure

Every startup has to decide on its structure from the word go. This structure will inevitably determine your taxes, legal liabilities, and the level of control you have over your business.

Your business structure could be a sole proprietorship, partnership, limited liability company (LLC), or corporation. Each structure type has its advantages and disadvantages, and the perfect choice for your startup will depend on various factors like:

- Your business goals

- How many owners does the business have

- How much risk you're willing to take

- Available financial resources

For instance, a sole proprietorship would be an excellent option if you're starting a small business and want complete control of the brand. Meanwhile, an LLC would suffice if you want to limit your liability while maintaining some control.

It'll help to consider your business's specific needs and circumstances before choosing a business structure. Also, it'll help to speak with legal professionals and other financial advisors on the merits and demerits of each option before making a choice.

Registering Your Business

Registering your business is one of the most crucial legal steps to take when launching your brand. It typically involves filing all necessary documents and paying the required fees to establish your brand as a legal entity within your state or country.

'What if I don't register my business?' you might be muttering already. Well, holding an unregistered business may not get you arrested (if you don't cross general regulations in special industries). However, registering your business can help you establish credibility with customers, suppliers, and potential investors.

Additionally, registering your business is an excellent way to protect your assets should another entity sue your brand.

The specific requirements to register a business vary from state to state or across countries. But it generally involves filing a business registration form and paying a fee. It sometimes also involves obtaining a business license, filing annual reports, or meeting other ongoing requirements to maintain the business's legal status.

Stay Informed of Other Legal Requirements

After choosing and registering your business structure, you want to stay updated with regulatory changes in your state or industry to ensure your business stays within the guidelines. Various ways to do this include regularly reviewing government websites, consulting with legal experts, and attending relevant conferences or seminars.

It can also help to join a professional association or networking group. These groups often share helpful information to help businesses remain legal and compliant.

Leverage Technology Solutions

Leveraging technology solutions and software tools can help businesses streamline their regulatory compliance. These software solutions can help you automate and monitor compliance requirements by providing insight to manage your obligations.

Some tools also automatically monitor legal and regulatory updates, providing insights into changes that could impact your business. Examples of helpful tools in this category include Social Mention, Evernote, RSS Feed Reader, and Visualping.io.

Seek Professional Advice

Seeking professional advice from lawyers, accountants, and regulatory experts can provide peace of mind and reduce overhead costs. Legal and regulatory experts can provide helpful information on the implications of every regulation or regulation change for your business and advise you on how to comply with them.

Embracing Failure and Iteration in Entrepreneurship

Failure is inevitable when developing a business. However, there's something fundamentally wrong with the use of the word. Most times, people use the word 'failure' to describe various experiences like setbacks, false starts, wrong moves, and errors.

However, rather than viewing failure in a catastrophic sense, entrepreneurs will do great to expect and tolerate these experiences while purposefully reiterating to gather new, relevant, and timely information.

Through iteration, startup founders work toward improving an idea rather than giving up on it. Additionally, by iterating, they route their experiences through a cycle of pivoting and adapting toward achieving the business's mission.

Let me show you some tips and strategies to help you develop a resilient, agile, and growth-inspiring mindset.

Measure and Experiment with Various Options and Hypotheses

Experimentation is at the center of innovation development. It allows you to explore various options and hypotheses while measuring their outcomes and impacts.

Tools like the Build-Measure-Learn loop or the Experiment Canvas can help you design and run experiments that test your assumptions and provide insightful feedback. It'll also help to define your goals, metrics, and success criteria before you collect the data you'll need to evaluate your results.

Share your findings with your team and other stakeholders. Hopefully, you'd be able to assess various available options to create a minimum viable product.

Assess Your Minimum Viable Product (MVP)

Test your assumptions and ideas with minimal resources and time via your lean prototype or minimum viable product (MVP). Learn what works and doesn't from the data and feedback you collect before floating the product or process.

Consider using tools like the Lean Canvas or the Business Model Canvas to map out various areas of your business, such as revenue streams, channels, customer segments, value propositions, and other vital metrics.

Persevere or Pivot

Decide whether to pivot an idea or hold back, depending on the results from your experiments and MVP assessment. Pivoting a plan means changing one or more aspects based on data from your experiments. Meanwhile, persevering tells you to continue with your current direction based on experimental evidence that you're on the right track.

Whether you persevere or pivot, it'll help you make this decision and tailor it based on your vision, goals, and validated learning rather than your emotions.

Learn from Failures

You probably already learned that the light bulb became what it is after 999 failed attempts. You probably already learned of Thomas Edison's response, the light bulb inventor, when asked about the 999 failed attempts.

Rather than claim to have failed almost a thousand times, Thomas Edison said he learned how *not* to make a light bulb.

That aptly sums up the lesson I'm about to emphasize.

Never be afraid of failing – failing fast and failing forward.

You can leverage tools like the Post-Mortem Analysis or the Five Whys to analyze the root causes of failure, spot key lessons, and identify helpful actions to improve your idea. Speak with consultants or other experienced professionals on the events, requesting their thoughts, suggestions, and recommendations for your next line of action.

Meanwhile, don't forget to celebrate your failures as milestones to learn new things. Rather than mourn your failures, iterate quickly.

Iterate Quickly

Iteration – or repetition – is a key to developing creative ideas. It allows you to refine and optimize your solutions based on feedback and lessons learned.

You'll do great to iterate quickly and often while prioritizing subsequent tasks and features based on their impact or value to your product. Lastly, don't forget to seek feedback and input from stakeholders and other users throughout the iteration process.

Maintain a Growth Mindset

Always keep a growth mindset that motivates you to make future-forward efforts and learn rather than being stationary or inactive. Moreover, maintaining a growth mindset allows you to embrace challenges, overcome obstacles, learn from feedback, and seek fresh opportunities.

One way to stoke your curiosity and maintain a growth mindset is to set realistic and achievable goals. Pursue these goals while reflecting on your achievements, seeking constructive criticism from others, and embracing lifelong learning.

Assessing Resources and Support

Your business resources or assets can include individuals, organizations, equipment, or buildings that can help you achieve your business goals. The available support for your business involves individuals and institutions that can contribute various resources to help facilitate or achieve your goals.

What resources are available to you? What support platforms are available to fund your needs? Asking the right questions can help you locate resource gaps that may eventually affect your future achievements. While helping you identify available support structures, asking helpful questions like these can help you locate the support you need to proceed.

Assessing the available resources and support for your business or career will help to identify areas you are uncertain about or grey areas that could turn south. Assess the potential risk impacts of these possible developments in your project and plan to avert or alleviate them.

Let's see how to develop a plan to identify local needs and resources to help you improve your community as logically and efficiently as possible.

Why You Need to Evaluate Your Business Assets and Resources

Assessing your business assets and resources can help you:

- Assess the feasibility of likely interventions

- Assess the need to acquire/mobilize assets

- Spot limiting factors, including those assets whose absence will prevent implementation

- Establish priorities for your business

List and Categorize Your Resources

Begin with mapping out the assets available around you. These could include products and services that can aid your business production process.

Next, identify relationships, partnerships, and other support structures that could positively impact your company. Think of these support systems as potential assets.

After gathering all necessary information, categorize and describe each asset concerning your business needs. Here are helpful categories to try.

- **People:** This includes detailing the number of staff on your team, their qualifications, expertise, skills, experience, and creativity.

- **Monetary:** Outline your cash flow, dedicated budgets, timescale, and potential sponsorship opportunities.

- **Physical:** includes buildings, locations, and more relevant to your organization.

- **Current products and services:** hotlines, mobile services, availability, and more.

- **Relationships:** internal and external relationships with employees, customers, communities, and funding providers.

- **Systems:** internal and external communication channels, helpful information, management, or institutions.

- **Intangibles:** including your ethics, values, work culture, knowledge, goodwill, and reputation.

Gather Your Outputs

The result of your audit could be an assets map, a resource audit report, or a chart that shows available support structures and resources.

This information will give you a clearer understanding of the available resources. Even more, it could point you to future actions toward acquiring additional resources.

Workbook 7

Join a mastermind group or create one. Share your goals with your mastermind group, ask thoughtful questions from your group, and note their observations to improve your career plans further.

Takeaway 7

Your successful entrepreneurship journey begins only when you cultivate an entrepreneurial mindset. An entrepreneurial mindset helps you assess your resources, identify business opportunities, market your brand, and create a successful business plan that fits them all.

It also helps you get your brand in front of the right audience, manage your cash flow successfully, and navigate any legalities. Lastly, successful entrepreneurs take failures as opportunities to iterate, reassess their strategies, and get back their focus on their ultimate career goals.

Part 3

Empowering Personal Growth

The story is told of a farmer's donkey that fell into a well. The animal cried piteously for hours while the farmer tried to think through the situation.

Finally, the farmer concluded the animal was old, wasn't worth retrieving, and should be covered up anyway. He invited all his neighbors to come around to help him. Each grabbed a shovel and started to shovel dirt into the well.

Upon realizing the impending doom, the donkey started crying horribly. Then, surprisingly, he quieted down.

A few shovels down the line, the farmer decided to look down the well and observe his donkey. He was surprised at what he saw.

The donkey did something amazing as each shoveled dirt hit his back. He would shake it off and take a step up.

The more the farmer's neighbors shoveled dirt on the animal, the more he would shake it off and climb a step higher. Soon enough, everyone was surprised as the old donkey stepped up over the edge of the well and happily trotted off.

Life will shovel dirt on you – all sorts of it. The escape route to getting out of the well is to shake it off and take a step higher.

No matter how deep a well you've been in or are in, giving up is no option. Shake the dirt off, and take a step up.

Are you ready to learn how to shake off the dirt, step over it, and become the best you can be in the face of threatening challenges?

Chapter 8

Overcoming Self-Doubt and Naysayers

'When life throws lemons at you, make lemonades, and sell it for a profit
– Anonymous

Boosting Self-confidence

Cultivating confidence and resilience

Why You Need to Be Resilient

Resilience is the ability to adapt and bounce back when things don't happen as planned. Resilient people don't dwell on failures. Instead, they acknowledge the situation, learn from their errors, and get going.

Health psychologists identify a strong link between the frequency and intensity of repeated or chronic daily life strains and one's overall health and illness.

According to a 2013 study, exposure to chronic, frequent negative emotions and a failure to process daily stress directly impact a person's mental health in the long term.

Individuals suffering from the lasting effects of trauma and adversity can readily develop prosocial behaviors that may speed up their healing if they can access resources that help them cope (or become resilient).

The bottom line is? A lack of resilience in the face of constant daily stress, trauma, or adversity has harmful psychological, health, and mental effects.

How to Develop Resilience

Meanwhile, according to the American Psychological Association (APA), resilience isn't a trait people have or don't have. Rather, resilience involves a set of behaviors, thoughts, and actions anyone can learn or develop.

Here are some helpful tips on developing resilience to weather life's challenges and bounce back into a better and stronger person.

1. **Act:** Make a move. Even small steps can add to your sense of accomplishment. Be proactive rather than reactive. It can help to start with something you feel confident you can do and ask for help when necessary. Remember, no one else can make a move for you.

2. **Stay Flexible:** Rather than condemn the development as a no-win event, gear toward an attitude of flexibility. Learn the art of positive compromise. And if you're facing pain that stops you from continuing, pat yourself on the back for your effort and the fact that you made efforts to improve your resilience. With time, you'll build more grit and improve your physical and mental health.

3. **Practice Optimism:** Train yourself to think positively and see opportunity often rather than dead-ends. For instance, see a half-full glass and not a half-empty cup.

4. **Leverage Support:** It's okay to ask for help when necessary. Asking for available support and showing a willingness to use it demonstrates a pro-social attitude. Remember, though, to offer support to others when they need it.

5. **Regard the Setback as a Temporary Development:** Nothing lasts forever, including disappointments, traumas, adversities, or pain. It'll help to navigate turbulent and emotionally trying times when you realize it is temporary, and things will improve as you actively participate in your healing process.

6. **Re-write Your Story:** Change your story to concentrate on the opportunities they revealed. Rather than focus on the negative aspects of your experience, concentrate on traits, skills, senses, and resources at your disposal. And that could include family, friends, or colleagues.

7. **Remain Grateful:** Cultivating a culture of gratitude helps you leverage a fundamental aspect of resilience and contentment in life. The more you develop gratitude, the more resilient you'll become.

8. **Relish in Other Victories:** Moments of failure can be extremely challenging. But this is the time to remind yourself of previous victories, successes, and challenging hurdles you overcame. Doing this helps remind you that you've overcome adversity before and'll do it again.

Developing Emotional Intelligence

Emotional intelligence, also called emotional quotient (EQ), is your ability to understand your emotions or others' feelings. It fuels your performance at work or personal life – but it begins with you.

It includes everything from self-control to confidence, empathy, optimism, and other social skills. Emotional intelligence helps you build stronger relationships, achieve your career and personal goals, and succeed at school or work.

Your intelligence quotient (IQ) might help you score high grades in school, but it's not enough of a quality to achieve success in life.

You probably already know some folks who aced all their courses yet are so socially inept or unsuccessful in their relationships. One of the things they lack is called emotional intelligence.

Emotional intelligence can also help you better connect with your actions and make more informed decisions about issues that matter most to you.

Leaders at various levels must build emotional intelligence to properly empathize with others, communicate effectively, and manage conflict.

Every teen needs four major skills to develop their emotional intelligence:

- Self-awareness

- Self-regulation

- Empathy; and

- Social Skills

We'll see these four skills and how to develop them in the following paragraphs.

Self-Awareness

Self-awareness lets people clearly understand their strengths, limitations, emotions, beliefs, and motivations. Teenage leaders and entrepreneurs who can quickly recognize and manage their emotions are better equipped to connect to others' feelings.

On the other hand, teams that lack self-awareness – who can't see a slip in performance – often make worse decisions that are less effective at managing conflict.

Conduct a SWOT analysis. Doing that helps you acknowledge your weaknesses and build trust and transparency among your team members. You're also more likely to develop your career when you identify areas where you need to improve toward advancing your career.

Self-Regulation

Self-regulation refers to how you manage your actions, feelings, and impulses. The more self-aware you are, the easier it is to regulate yourself. For instance, if you recognize your feelings and why you have them, you can effectively chart a proper response to them.

The key is to avoid emotional outbursts or overreacting to almost anything that comes your way. Here are helpful tactics to help you improve your self-regulation.

- **Pause before Responding:** Take time to pause before replying to any event or action. It could be as straightforward as taking deep breaths or waiting for 20 seconds till your feelings get out of your thought-streams.

- **Take a Step Away:** Sometimes, you might need to leave the conversation temporarily. It's okay to leave the room when the emotions are rushing. Take a walk, drink some water, or call a friend. Doing these things can prevent you from sending a harmful email or lashing out at your team.

- **Understand your emotions:** It'll help to jot down the feelings that caused the distress. Soon, you'll start identifying patterns that suggest actions that trigger you. That way, the next time a similar event occurs, you'll be better prepared to handle it positively.

Practicing self-regulation can help you better respond to events and avoid anything that could hamper the good name you've built for your business.

Empathy

Empathy is one of the top leadership skills in need today. Empathy shows you understand other people's experiences and emotions. Research shows that leaders who excel at listening to others and respond empathetically perform at least 40 percent more in coaching, planning, and decision-making.

Other research shows that companies that prioritize empathy enjoy increased revenue, employee retention, and productivity.

Actively listening to your employees and understanding their wants and needs can help you build trust, boost engagement, and even lead the team through tough times. Moreover, the more your team feels appreciated, the more invested they'll be in your organization and contribute to higher morale and stronger company culture.

Meanwhile, empathy goes beyond the goodwill you extend to others. Don't forget to show *empathy* to yourself too.

That means it's okay to cry when things go south. But it's also okay to forget disappointments and concentrate on the good things that make you happy.

Social Skills

For instance, a socially aware leader can come to the office a day after a board meeting to find nearly everyone on his staff rolled with frenzied looks and uncertain postures. Without stopping at his discovery, the socially-aware leader will ease the pressure in the air with an assuring pose that gets most of his team members motivated and smiling again.

Social skills refer to how you perceive your emotions and interact with others. Keeping in touch with your emotions helps you connect to others and the world around you.

Social skills also help you differentiate friend from foe, accurately measure someone else's interest in you, manage stress, and better balance your nervous system via social communication. They also help you feel loved and happy at all times.

Remember, none of these skills are explicitly taught in any college or high school. If anything, let that show you that one of the most critical skill sets for success in business or a career doesn't require a college degree.

Overcoming Imposter Syndrome

'I'm not as great as people think.'

'Soon enough, everyone will find out I'm a fraud and place me where I truly belong.'

Have you ever had these thoughts?

Well, that's the imposter phenomenon speaking. Around 33% of young people suffer from it. And 82% of people have suffered from imposter syndrome at one point or another throughout their lifetime.

They often think they didn't earn what they achieved. Despite being smart, skilled, and capable professionals who deserve the commendations and praise they receive – or even more – people suffering from imposter syndrome feel like frauds.

However, if your successes and achievements came through your knowledge, hard work, and preparation, and you still feel insufficient, you're probably suffering from the imposter phenomenon.

Psychologists coined the term in the late '70s to note three critical attributes of imposter syndrome:

- Thinking people have an exaggerated view of their abilities

- The constant tendency to downplay their achievements

- The fear of being exposed as a fraud

The imposter syndrome is common in workplaces.

But it can also manifest in relationships and every other aspect of life.

It typically shows up when people take on new roles and responsibilities and can result in feelings of self-doubt, guilt, and anxiety.

People who experience imposter syndrome may eventually sabotage their success if they continue obsessing over little mistakes – or even, on the other end, work twice as hard to prove themselves.

Neither extreme position benefits your emotional, mental, or professional well-being.

Sadly, people with this phenomenon can often do so much to hide their feelings, reducing their chances of future success.

Do I Have the Imposter Syndrome?

Many people often overlook the signs of imposter syndrome in their daily lives. Here are common thoughts, feelings, and actions people suffering from this phenomenon can often relate to:

- They feel 'lucky' even though they prepared well and worked hard

- They find it difficult to accept praise

- They apologize for themselves when they didn't do anything wrong

- They hold themselves to often impossibly high standards

- The fear of failure often feels paralyzing

- They avoid expressing confidence because they think others will see it as being obnoxious

- They turn down opportunities for growth or visibility at work

- People close to you say you aren't as confident as you used to be

- They're convinced they're not enough

It'll help to pay attention to your language choices during conversations with others and moments you spend talking to yourself.

Does it feel uncomfortable admitting the praise of others or talking about your success?

It'll help to conduct some reflective thinking on where these thoughts originate from and what it means to your career.

If you're starting a new role, a new relationship, or living in a new environment, overcoming imposter syndrome might seem impossible.

However, if you fail to keep it under check now, it can negatively impact your performance, lead to burnout, and eventually depression in the long term.

Worse still, imposter syndrome can lead to increased anxiety and depression, reduced risk-taking, and career burnout.

4 Tips to Help You Overcome Imposter Syndrome

1. Understand that You Are Not Alone

If you discover traits of imposter syndrome in yourself, you must realize that many successful people, regardless of their sexes, have built great careers while coping with this phenomenon.

Multiple award-winning actor Donald Cheadle Jr. once owned up to his imposter syndrome tendencies.

'All I can see is everything I am doing wrong that is a sham and a fraud,' the two-time Grammy award winner once said.

Meanwhile, Maya Angelou, a former author, poet, and civil rights activist who had written eleven books, once admitted to the imposter syndrome too.

'Uh, oh, they're going to find out now. I've run a game on everybody, and they're going to find me out.'

2. Differentiate Fear from Humility

Being humble about your hard work, successes, and achievements is one thing. But feeling overcome with fear because of them is not the way to go.

There's a thin line between feeling worthy and feeling *entitled*. It's possible to feel worthy without being entitled. And overcoming imposter syndrome often involves finding a balance between both worlds.

You can be humble, open to feedback, and gracious in your mannerisms – without feeling like a fraud.

3. Put Aside Your Inner Perfectionist

Perfectionism can often pose a major roadblock to productivity. Unsurprisingly, it can also prevent you from quickly overcoming imposter syndrome.

Like Maya or Donald in our earlier real-life examples, many people who suffer from imposter syndrome are high achievers. They're people who set impossibly high standards for themselves while committing to do their best and be the best.

But perfectionism will contribute more to your imposter syndrome than make you a more productive or healthy professional.

Often, you're likely feeling insufficient because you're comparing yourself with some 'perfect' outcome or person that's either unrealistic or simply impossible.

4. Be Nice to You

Negative self-talk is a bad habit that can severely influence your stress and anxiety levels.

Avoid berating yourself with negative messages like, 'You're not smart enough.' 'You're not good enough' or 'You're a fraud.'

Be nice to yourself in the way you talk to you about you. Doing so can help you avoid stress and anxiety and build the courage to accomplish more rewarding tasks.

Be on the lookout to catch yourself whenever a negative thought runs through your mind. Suppose you find yourself saying, 'I don't deserve this.' Turn it around and ask yourself, 'What steps did I take, and what did I overcome to get to this spot?'

Then you're ready to talk to yourself in positive, self-affirming words about your future goals.

Dealing with Criticism and Rejection

No matter how poorly or well you perform – criticism and rejection are two sides of the coin life shows to every one of us. We've all received disappointing remarks or comments, but it never seems to get softer.

Whether you're a creative who wants to put their work out there, an entrepreneur who wants to win grant proposals or a leader who loves to have their audience's heart and hands, get ready to learn how to handle rejection and criticism when they come.

Don't be so fearful of criticism or rejection that you keep your creativity, business idea, or message bottled up.

Award-winning Canadian poet Margaret Atwood knew well how to handle criticism when her most notable work, *The Handmaid's Tale,* received some negative reviews.

She said, 'If you believe the good reviews, you're also going to have to believe the bad reviews.'

Ouch, tough skin, that is!

Now, *your* tough skin won't develop overnight. But you can grow tough skin against life's criticisms and rejections when you practice what I'll show you in this subsection.

Here you go!

Admit to Your Feelings

Rejection and criticism are unpleasant – and you have to admit it. That's because we all need to acknowledge and accept grief or pain before healing.

So, suppose you receive an unwanted remark from an audience when presenting a message or idea. The first thing you'd do when you leave that platform is to state loudly how you feel. It could be somewhere you're alone in your office or room so you don't disturb others.

Stand in the middle of that room. Yell, 'That hurt!' or 'I didn't expect that!' Whatever. Whatever to express your unhappiness.

Once you acknowledge that it's unpleasant, you're in a better place – for two reasons. One, you've been able to let loose some negativity through verbal expression. Well, you might not believe this. But voicing your pain (or even screaming at the top of your lungs) can help ease the pain.

Mind you, you don't want to do this in public where doing so can give people a wrong perspective about you. It's perfectly okay to pause, take a breath, or walk away so you don't overreact (EQ, remember?).

Next, give yourself a pat on the back (there mustn't be a justification for it). Yes, you don't *have* to do it. Whether or not you can currently find anything good about the effort someone else criticized, no one's pat would suffice if you choose not to give yourself a thumbs up!

Show yourself some compassion, and finding the courage to move on will be much easier.

Understand the Difference

After showing yourself some self-love and clearing (or easing) your mental health, it's time to do some good thinking.

Understand the difference between rejection and criticism.

Rejection might be a clear, firm, 'no,' but criticism isn't always a firm no.

Often, rejection comes immediately after criticism. Rejection from a publisher, company, investor, or audience may or may not come with any feedback. Sometimes, you're left to wonder what led to the rejection.

On the other hand, criticism comes in various forms. It could be constructive or destructive.

Constructive criticism is helpful and offers actionable and specific suggestions in a feedback form. On the other hand, destructive criticism would offer little or no helpful suggestions.

Find the Silver Lining in Criticism

As your confidence returns gradually, it's time to learn to accept the feedback and find the silver lining in each comment.

Don't see this stage of your recovery process as a choice but a necessity. Of course, not every criticism or rejection will offer great nuggets; some will.

Find the beauty in your criticisms – and embrace it.

Decide Whether or Not You'll Respond

When emotions run high, you might be tempted to respond suddenly or spontaneously. An emotionally intelligent person won't *demean themselves*, using the words of the Novelist Truman Capote about this subject, by talking back to a critic.

When you choose to respond, remember to thank them for the feedback and concentrate on the facts of the criticism, where you can ask for suggestions for further improvements.

Don't Stop Trying

Never let criticism or rejection stop you from pursuing your dreams.

It doesn't matter if it's your first or tenth rejection. Keep putting your work, ideas, or content out.

If you receive them, let other people's suggestions about your profile or work motivate you to adjust your craft, not end it.

Look out for various reasons to remind yourself why you love what you do. It can help to travel down the line to see what sparked your creativity, idea, or hope in the first place. It could help renew your interest and even spur you into a new and rewarding direction!

Join or Leverage Your Communities

Do you have a group of friends who do what you do or something closely related? Then you're in good company.

Otherwise, consider joining a community. Online communities help you improve your skill, craft, idea, or overall profile. They can even recommend a new audience that might like your work or provide a helpful referral.

Finally, communities can help you stay more accountable to your set goals and dreams.

Building a supportive network

Being a solopreneur doesn't mean you have to go it all alone. Everyone needs people in their lives they can count on in pleasant and unpleasant times. You need a supportive network in your personal lives as well as your business.

Your support network can make the difference between feeling like you're out in the jungle on your own and feeling you have a team of advisers, friends, and partners who can be there for you when you're confused, down, and out – or available to share a drink to celebrate victories when they come.

A support network can also help you transition into other areas of your career or life. And they may include family, friends, colleagues, teachers, mentors, or acquaintances. Here are helpful tips for building a supportive network to support your career goals.

Recognize the Supports Presently in Your Life

You want to begin with recognizing the family, friends, colleagues, teachers, or mentors currently in your life. Create a list of people you know and the opportunities or strengths they can offer you. While one person might be a great resume reviewer, another might have helpful, professional relationships that may benefit you.

Doing this helps you appreciate the network you already have and positions you to leverage them wisely toward advancing your career goals. Additionally, auditing your current support network helps you recognize the support you *need* to maximize your goals.

Attend Events and Conferences

Attend events that allow you to get in touch with new people who can support your personal, career, or entrepreneurial development. These events could include career fairs, community meetings, workshops, or even birthday parties.

Introduce yourself to people you think might be helpful to your achieving your goals. Keep their contact information or portfolio in a notebook, and plan to contact them after the first meeting.

Avoid Trying to Withdraw from Places You Haven't Made Withdrawals

It's unfair to email people asking them to mentor you without telling them what you could offer them. A little gesture, like taking a prospect out to coffee or sharing a portrait you made for them, shows you believe in a mutually beneficial relationship.

Tina Wells, a business coach and board member of the Young Entrepreneur Council, shared about a friend who built their entire business by taking people for lunch. This friend succeeded in taking some important people out for lunch, who eventually funded his business.

If you asked Tina's friend about his secret to success, he'd most likely tell you he simply asked people to lunch.

Join Helpful Associations

Look out for associations that provide support to people in your field. You might be surprised how many industries or niches have associations and other support structures that may help.

For instance, if you're a female, joining a local branch of the National Association of Women Business Owners or a similar organization in your country can be of great relief and support. Moreover, these associations can also provide a network of peers, product discounts, referrals, and other perks that can help you hone your craft.

Create a Mastermind Group

While joining larger and nationwide associations can help you gain visibility and connect you to the crème de la crème in your field, creating a small group of professionals in your area can create something Napoleon Hill called a 'mastermind' group.

Napoleon Hill first coined the concept of a mastermind group in 1925 in his book *The Law of Success.* He expounded on this concept in the all-time best-selling *Think and Grow Rich.*

A mastermind group is a peer-to-peer mentoring group where members provide support and advice to solve one another's problems. It's like a gathering of like-minded people who meet frequently in small groups.

Your mastermind group is a great place to support, encourage, and learn from one another's experiences and goals. It's also a place to hold one another accountable to well-defined goals.

Speak with your contacts at your school, religious groups, trade groups, or professional associations. Inform them about the need to create a mastermind group. Who knows? You might not need to create one; they might ask you to join theirs!

Reframing Success Beyond Degrees

Success must be self-defined. Even more, it *should* be defined to reflect every area of your life.

Here's what I mean.

People have always defined success using money and power as their leading reasons for wanting success. Similarly, being overworked and always busy has become an achievement in itself.

You've probably heard the phrase, 'hustle 'till you no longer have to introduce yourself.'

Even when a business takes eight to ten hours each working day, people will likely ask what else you're doing with your time.

It feels like you win more rewards as you spend more hours at work. As long as you can work long enough, hard enough, or fast enough, your desired result is always achievable.

But seeing success this way is particularly detrimental.

Fine, you want to succeed, and to a large extent, some stress levels are necessary to perform maximally.

But when your stress levels start getting into chronic levels, it can cause a series of physical and mental disorders, which could eventually end up in complete burnout.

Your business or career can quickly take over your life as it grows. Sadly, burnout and chronic stress affect your productivity with time, which makes maintaining success no longer achievable.

An Emotional Investment

Whether you choose to or otherwise, starting your business or even pursuing a career is a huge emotional investment, and the journey can be filled with financial uncertainty.

You're often so immersed in your pursuit that it can be hard to step back and switch off.

What about missed opportunities or clients?

Missed opportunities can bring with them so much guilt or fear that further evokes extreme decisions. On the one hand, they can force you to cow away from future opportunities, throw in the towel, or reduce your career expectations. On the other hand, it could make you dread taking the slightest break from work so you don't miss further opportunities.

Not to mention the lack of self-belief or critical self-talk that barges against your mind after seriously coming short of your expectations.

Often, the world celebrates successful entrepreneurs or leaders for having laser focus. However, the seemingly positive attribute can be a challenge if your dedication and commitment develop into an obsession.

It could mean sacrificing things that should help you grow emotional intelligence or social awareness, such as:

- Going out with family and friends

- Getting enough sleep

- Making time to rest, or

- Prioritizing self-care

Pay Attention to Your Emotions

Don't ignore signs that you're possibly heading toward exhaustion. Here are some helpful questions to ask from time to time about your emotional health.

- Am I struggling to fall asleep and remain asleep?

- Have my loved ones shown concern about my behavior?

- Am I often exhausted?

- Am I more anxious about my career or business than before?

- Do I find it challenging to make decisions or get overwhelmed easily?

- Do I do things that make me joyful?

- Do I find it challenging to concentrate?

One way to ensure you're emotionally fit to fight for your career or business is to assess the middle line, the equilibrium. You want to reevaluate what success means to you.

And that begins with being fully focused and mentally involved enough to appreciate your achievements. Evaluate tasks based on what happiness or joy they bring you.

Acknowledge how far you've come, accept areas you need to develop, and plan toward fulfilling the clear goals for your future.

Monitoring Your Health

You want to prioritize your health to ensure your body and mind are in the best shape they can be. Whether you want it or not, you couldn't complete a balanced success definition without maintaining quality relationships.

These helpful relationships will be there for you when obstacles arise, you're nearing burnout, or life *happens* to you.

While I don't promise you'll always get a perfect balance, regularly nurturing your physical, mental, and emotional well-being can help you create the best foundations to succeed.

By this point, I'm sure you discovered I didn't mention anything about degrees in this subsection.

Do you know why?

College education *per se* doesn't make people *succeed* in a balanced way. It doesn't promise you emotional health or mental wellness. It doesn't even promise money or fame, either!

As you may have seen throughout this book, many industries today require short courses, skills, and apprenticeships you can gain without spending a fortune in college. There are also other fields, like IT, where employers would gladly employ anyone with enough skills or experience in an area or willing to learn the ropes of the trade.

University education may not be for everyone. And if you choose not to pursue one, then search diligently for industries or professions that can allow you to become everything you want to be without giving a hoot about a degree.

Workbook 8

Join a mastermind group or create one. Share your goals with your mastermind group, ask thoughtful questions from your group, and note their observations to improve your career plans further.

Takeaway 8

First, ditch the imposter syndrome.

You haven't run *a game* on anyone. And you possibly won't.

You *deserve* attention, appreciation, and rewards for your skill, hard work, and constructive relationships.

Again, it's okay to scream out loud (in the center of your room, alone!) after getting criticisms or rejections.

Find the silver lining in your rejections or criticisms, respond gracefully (if at all) to critics, and finally, leverage your initial motivation and community to find enough strength to sail through the coming season.

Chapter 9

Making an Impact in Your Community

'The world is a dangerous place, not because of those who do evil, but because of those who look on and do nothing
– Albert Einstein

Amplify Your Positive Influence

Understanding Social Entrepreneurship and Civic Engagement

As you grow in business and impact, you'll quickly learn that people often care less about what you know or even have until they're sure you care.

Perhaps this quote from Professor Muhammad Yunus, a Bangladeshi social entrepreneur, will help drive this point home quickly:

'I'm encouraging young people to become social business entrepreneurs and contribute to the world rather than just making money. Making money is no fun. Contributing to and changing the world is a lot more fun.'

Who's a social entrepreneur, anyway?

A social entrepreneur pursues novel applications that have the potential to solve community-based problems. These individuals choose to take the risk and effort required to create positive societal changes through their solutions.

As David Bornstein, author of How to Change the World, puts it:

'Social entrepreneurs identify resources where people only see problems. For instance, they see the underprivileged as the solution rather than the passive beneficiary.'

Social entrepreneurs go beyond doing business with the sole aim of earning profit. Instead, they seek to implement widespread improvements in society.

However, they *do* make a profit. Being financially savvy is critical for social entrepreneurs to succeed and serve their communities for long. While most social entrepreneurs begin with modest goals that help them prioritize their mission, many eventually can achieve financial success just like conventional entrepreneurs.

Types of Social Entrepreneurs

1. Community Social Entrepreneur

A community social entrepreneur usually concentrates on a small community, usually its host community. These types of entrepreneurs are less concerned about what they do. Instead, they focus on how their activities will benefit their community.

2. Non-Profit Social Entrepreneur

Non-profit social entrepreneurs are the most common categories of social entrepreneurs. These social entrepreneurs have stated goals that benefit people within or outside their immediate environment or community.

They often operate very similarly to conventional businesses. However, the net profits obtained from these non-profit organizations are often returned to pursue their socially-forward mission. And that could include anything from funding beneficiaries to developing the system to serve the world better.

3. Transformational Social Entrepreneur

As start-ups grow, they tend to graduate into becoming transformational social entrepreneurs. Transformational social entrepreneurs go beyond the non-profit social entrepreneur by extending their mission from a single program to help others benefit in multiple areas.

The transformational social entrepreneurship organization is often much richer and broader, with several rules and regulations. A helpful example of a non-profit that has achieved this feat is Goodwill Incorporated, a 501 organization that provides job training, employment placement services, and other community-based programs to people who have barriers to their employment.

4. Global Social Entrepreneur

Global social entrepreneurs have broken all border or geographical limits. They work to solve broader social challenges like poverty, depression, hunger, or inequality.

Often, even though the issues they tackle are often deep-rooted and found everywhere, the global social entrepreneur works to solve these issues in a specific region. A helpful example of this is the Bill & Melinda Gates Foundation, a global social enterprise that has helped find vaccinations for various diseases.

As you may have guessed already, what started as a community social enterprise today may become a global one.

Suppose a social entrepreneur discovers a community around them lacks access to fresh water. They could provide freshwater services by constructing new wells. With time, the social entrepreneur could extend their services to reach communities that lack stable utilities.

6 Elements of Social Entrepreneurship

Social entrepreneurs often work through each of these six elements. Each of these elements is vital to overcoming the challenges social entrepreneurs face and helping them maximize their impact in their world.

Making an Impact in Your Community

1. People-Centered

Social entrepreneurs center activities around people. They begin by identifying the needy people around them.

Without clearly defining who they want to serve, a social entrepreneur will face difficulty defining the scope of their activities.

This event may involve people in their immediate environment or people within a specific demographic (i.e., people with a low income). This creates a clear path or vision for the budding organization.

2. Problem-Solving

Social entrepreneurs usually spot a problem they want to fix in their target demographic. For instance, a social entrepreneur might try to defeat homelessness in under-aged children in their city. The solution the social entrepreneur brings, then, involves providing housing facilities.

3. Planning

Once they identify the people and the problem they want to solve, the next stage involves devising a plan to solve the problem.

This plan would include a viable business plan that helps it operate as a successful entity. It should also include how the enterprise intends to generate funding (from internal or external sources)and remain financially sustainable.

4. Priorities

Social entrepreneurs often set out to solve major social issues and are often short of the required resources to solve the problems they try to solve.

That's why they need to prioritize the solutions they try to offer, their scale and mode of operations, as well as plans to scale their business.

5. Minimum Viable Products

One way social entrepreneurs work to maximize limited resources is to test-run solutions in small communities before scaling them. This action involves creating minimum viable products (MVPs), services, or activities.

They also work toward testing how various sources of funding and resources can help them achieve their goals. Lastly, creating prototypes can help social entrepreneurs encourage potential investors who may appreciate the minimized project.

6. Execution

MVP experiments tell the social entrepreneur what requires changes and what should be reflected in the final product. They then move to execute the ideas they learned, continually monitoring the scaled-up service or product for better ways to improve it.

Leveraging Tech for Social Change

Not only has technology experienced a series of changes over the decades, but it's also an effective tool for driving change worldwide. Tech has reshaped various segments of everyday life, from tourism to agriculture, retail, culture, entertainment, and even governance.

However, as people relish the benefits of human innovation and creativity to profit them, they must leverage technological advancement for purposes other than *themselves*.

I'm making a case for tech products that go beyond impacting just one sector to reach the larger population.

Thankfully, this book isn't asking you to pioneer a path no one else has toured. A growing number of companies are already emphasizing the need to leave a legacy and create a lasting social impact worldwide.

They may be passionate about creating an impact that will reach the less privileged in today's world. Otherwise, they're concerned about addressing global issues like inequality, climate change, and deforestation.

However, there's something past efforts to drive social change don't have. It's the technology of the future.

Now, I'm going to explain myself in a moment.

Bill Gates might be creating vaccines to cure illnesses like COVID-19 or polio, and Goodwill might be trying to make jobs more available to disadvantaged people.

But neither Bill Gates nor Goodwill is pursuing their social impacts using yet-to-be-developed technology. And that's understandable.

Wait – you don't have to invent any new technology or innovation no one has ever used.

Instead, I'm pickling your interest and readiness to leverage the next set of tech advancements for a greater good than profiting you or your business.

Do you get my drift now?

Former President Barrack Obama might be at the forefront of leadership development worldwide, and every other great person pushing for social change is doing their best. But *you*, not them, have a higher chance of witnessing and leveraging future technology for social change.

That means, among many other things, that you must be ready to learn how to learn and master some of the effective ways to leverage technology for social change. You want to learn the fundamentals of social entrepreneurship and how to overcome the challenges of the social sector.

Steps to Effectively Leveraging Technology for Social Change

1. Identify the Problem and the Solution

Regardless of the social impact you want to make or the field you want to make, the first step to leveraging technology for social change is to identify the problem you want to solve. Follow your problem statement with one or more solutions you intend to offer.

To effectively do this, you want to understand the root causes, the stakeholders, the context, and the impact of the challenges. Then, you want to audit existing solutions and current gaps in the sector or market you desire to impact.

After auditing existing solutions, you might be ready to float your proposals and validate them with your target beneficiaries and recipients. Test your assumptions and hypotheses against hard facts or real-world experiments.

That said, you want to leverage the right technologies at this point to help with tasks like data collection, analysis, feedback, prototyping, and iteration. All these are fundamental actions to ultimately introduce your novel or creative innovation to make a social impact in the world around you.

2. Choose the Appropriate Technology

The second step involves choosing the appropriate technology that can help deliver your desired results or solutions. Doing this would involve assessing various factors of the considered tech options, including their:

- Accessibility
- Availability
- Affordability
- Appropriateness for users

It'll also help to consider the technology's potential benefits, risks, costs, and trade-offs, and how it relates to your social mission and core values.

Again, you'll also need existing technologies to scale your solutions and improve their efficiency, creativity, reach, and differentiation from other available initiatives.

3. Build a Sustainable Business Model

The next step in leveraging technology for social change involves building a sustainable business model for your solution. Remember, social entrepreneurs may not work *for* profit, but they must also be financially sustainable and should be profitable in the long run.

You want to define your value proposition, revenue streams, cost structure, customer segments, and channels. It'll also help to measure your model's social and financial performance while adjusting to your discoveries.

Remember, you'll always need existing technologies to deliver new or innovative tech solutions. Here's the place to bring in tech tools to help with your market research, customer acquisition, product pricing and distribution, and remittances.

4. Engage with Stakeholders

Engage with beneficiaries, customers, partners, funders, employees, and volunteers related to your solution. Effectively communicate your vision, mission, and desired impact with them, building trust and relationships with each stakeholder.

Collaborate with them, create alongside them, and learn with them. That way, you can leverage their skills, resources, and networks to execute your solutions effectively.

Here, technology can help you with branding, marketing, advocating, and educating others about your solutions.

5. Adapt Your Solutions

As you begin executing your desired tech solutions for social change, you'll discover new environmental situations that might differ from what you used in culturing your prototype. These changes could include social, economic, political, and technological trends or challenges.

When you notice this, it's time to adapt. It's time to monitor, evaluate, and learn from your results, using the required insights to improve your solution and operations.

Meanwhile, it'll also help to anticipate changes in your target populations or environment and your response to these changes as they come. As a tech-savvy social entrepreneur, you're prepared to innovate in the face of uncertain developments, complex occurrences, and positive or unwanted disruptions.

During this phase, technology can help you manage, analyze, visualize, and report data. Tech solutions can also help you with improving your decision-making processes.

6. Be Ethical in Your Approach

The final step to leveraging technology for social change is to be ethical and responsible in using and deploying technology. Whatever solution you provide, respect your stakeholders' rights, privacy, and dignity. Protect them from harm or exploitation, either directly via your solutions or the processes that help to deliver them.

Here's where you want to onboard tech tools to help you with compliance, governance, accountability, and ethical design.

Volunteering and Community Service Opportunities

Volunteering and various community service opportunities are another great way to give back to the world around you.

Now, if you've been wondering what services or projects you can take up to help people in your area, this subsection covers you.

I've made your task less stressful by outlining 25 volunteering and community service opportunities that may lie unexploited.

Let's check them out.

25 Ways to Volunteer and Service Your Community, Wherever You Are

1. Help out at a Homeless Shelter

According to a National Law Center on Homelessness & Poverty report, about 3.5 million Americans sleep in homeless shelters, transitional housing, and public areas where people shouldn't sleep (like bridges, bus stops, etc.). Spending time with people going through a sorry state can make an immense difference.

Cook food for the older residents, clean the community kitchen/common area, or teach the children a random skill or language.

2. Assist Hospitals

You don't need an educational background to volunteer at a hospital. Hospital stays can be quite hectic. You can help relieve tension in patients and even health professionals by playing an instrument in the lobby or just *anything* you can to entertain the entire hospital.

Who knows? Your jovial and lively presence in the hospital can help return smiles to a sick child's face or make an exhausted nurse regain her strength.

3. Volunteer at an Animal Shelter

Now, if you've been seeking volunteering opportunities that don't directly involve people, an animal shelter might be the place for you.

That's because animal shelters almost always seek volunteers to feed, groom, or entertain lively animals. Meanwhile, helping cats, dogs, and other animals become more friendly and sociable increases their chances of a successful adoption.

4. Gift Christmas Presents

Various organizations let you share boxes of gifts to underprivileged children worldwide. Christmas is a great time to help others without traveling to visit them in person. Beautiful gift ideas include shoes, coloring books, crayons, chapter books, and more.

5. Package Meals

Like Christmas presents, various organizations around the US make it easy for high school students to package meals for people suffering from hunger. These meals often include appropriate nourishment to help children grow into healthier adults.

6. Help Out at a Library

Do you enjoy books or a quiet environment? A library might be the perfect place for you to give back to others.

Volunteering at a library helps you organize books and find new books to include in your to-be-read list. And if helping the kids sounds like a fulfilling adventure to you, take some time to teach them, read to them, and recommend helpful materials to them.

7. Support the Red Cross

The Red Cross offers disaster relief, blood donations, and more to disadvantaged communities worldwide. Moreover, volunteering with the Red Cross also provides some experience in the medical field while allowing you to help needy people.

Seeing devastated communities can be challenging. But you could participate in fostering their recovery. You may also meet new friends along the way.

8. Play at the YMCA

Everyone knows that staying at the YMCA is fun. You can serve as a volunteer while having fun with your local YMCA.

The Geneva-based nonprofit organization is where you can interact with kids and serve as their role model. It also lets you work in various interest areas, from playing sports to coaching an athletic team or teaching a musical instrument.

9. Donate Unwanted Items

Not everyone has the privilege to have the ability to purchase needed items at their full price. One way to help them is by donating unwanted or unused items to local charities and women's shelters. These organizations, in turn, donate your unwanted items to thrift stores where others can purchase them at a highly reduced rate.

10. Coach a Kids' Sports Team

Are you skilled in a sport enough to coach younger folks to learn what you know? Consider coaching a kids' sports team. You could share your passion with the kids while acting as a mentor or role model to them. Who knows? Volunteering to these kids might unlock another aspect of you, the sports, or your career you never knew existed.

11. Volunteer at the Local Park

Do you love green spaces and would love to protect them from invasion, defacement, or harm? Volunteer to pick up trash, maintain trails, or help organize and run park events. Besides protecting the aesthetics and health of the environment, you could also treat yourself to an amazing outdoor time.

12. Host Events in Your Community

Hosting community events helps you hone your event-planning skills while putting a smile on others' faces.

Host a bake sale, call for a holiday meal, open a competitive book driver, or a study group. Publicly hosting events and sharing your creativity with others can help uplift and revitalize your community.

13. Make Items for People in the Area

If you've ever received – or given – one, you could tell that handmade gifts connect differently. Well, if you don't think it's a particularly great gift to receive from someone else, many people and places would appreciate a handmade gift from you.

Knit scarves or hats for elderly people in shelters; bake cookies and snacks for food pantries; make Christmas cards for your neighbors; or design a community mural. You can never tell how impactful or beneficial your gift would be.

14. Fix Things in Your Community

Sometimes, one of the best services you can provide to others revolves around doing something worthwhile to care for places you love.

How about helping your neighbors with repairs or fixing clothes and stuffed toys? Placing campfire safety plaques near campsites or sprucing up a run-down playground?

You could also help a neighbor or community organization paint a fence or give IT help to local adults.

15. And Many More!

Still looking for the perfect fit? You can check online for various volunteering organizations or websites that aggregate various community service opportunities near you. International Volunteer HQ, Love Volunteers, VolunteerMatch, the Broader View Volunteers, or almost any public institution near you would have something you like.

Initiating Grassroots Projects for Meaningful Impacts

You may have considered participating in volunteering or community service opportunities others create. And that's great, immensely recommendable.

But you may also have considered initiating a grassroots project to impact your community. You may not find a program that best suits your goals for social change or impact. However, a challenge you may face as you ponder on launching a project is how to do what you want.

Moreover, launching your grassroots program lets you hone skills like project management, creativity, people management, event planning, fundraising (yes, it's a skill!), and many more. Follow these steps to build grassroots projects from scratch and make your voice heard where it matters – in the minds and hearts of people around you.

1. Know the Right Time to Begin Your Grassroots Advocacy Program

Only launch your grassroots program when your team is ready to unite all resources to pursue a social cause. A great lead could be waiting for an 'aha' moment – when a significant bill gets released, a major disaster breaks out, or some scathing statistics get published.

Launching at these 'high points' moments can put your advocacy program right at the top of the minds of potential advocates.

It could also help to engage various aspects of your industry or field before launching out. These various segments range from association members to beneficiaries, suppliers, and other industry-allied stakeholders. Doing so can help increase your program's influence with policymakers, top entrepreneurs, and leading figures in your community, state, or even nation.

2. Create Your First-Year Roadmap

A one-year roadmap showcases your readiness to float your advocacy program until it makes a meaningful and sustainable impact on your environment.

It'll help to sketch out the work you see ahead of your team or break them into tasks or quarters. Meanwhile, ensure your first-year roadmap includes clear goals and upfront metrics for measuring their achievements.

This might also include numbering how many advocates you want to recruit in the first year or how much percentage of your organization you'd want to participate as advocates. Your first-year plan could also include what and how many tasks or advocacy actions each team member would execute within that period.

Your roadmap gives your team or association a north star on where all plans are headed. It can also help boost your leadership profile and increase your team's interest in the project. Finally, setting the right baseline metrics to measure each action can help you assess various advocacy actions and plan for future events in subsequent years.

3. Find a Platform to Mobilize Advocates and Help Them Take Action

Thanks to technology, many mobile-friendly grassroots advocacy software platforms let you advertise your association's goals and grow its membership. Helpful tools include texting and Facebook integration.

The right platform isn't only visible to your target audience. It should also lower the barrier to action for potential advocates. Your advocacy platform should help people readily learn about your organization, read about pending matters, and take action without switching between software or platforms.

It can also help them share their personalized or forwarded campaigns with friends, co-workers, and family. Thankfully, helpful advocacy software can help you do all these.

Mind you, technologies like this often come at some cost. However, you want to prove the potential ROI of these tools to your association's stakeholders and leadership. Demonstrating the value of this software to them, especially if it displays real-time data on popular campaigns, the number of actions others took, or the number of new advocates that joined your team in a year.

That way, your team would likely appreciate the required funds that go into leveraging tech tools and possibly even support the use of advanced or more helpful tools.

4. Develop Your Advocacy Brand and Promotional Strategy

Your advocacy brand strategy outlines how you intend to create messages, market, and advertise your brands. The ideal strategy must be relevant to a large group of individuals beyond just your team members who can help support your advocacy efforts.

Your brand strategy should circle your mission. For instance, suppose your brand wants to concentrate on empowering people to speak out and seek solutions; ensure your promotional strategies carry a touch of this goal.

That said, developing a narrow mission makes it easy for others to understand, remember, share, and recognize your brand. Whether you're posting emails or on social media, encourage your audience to sign up as grassroots social advocates. Work with internal or external graphic designers or teams to create beautiful and creative content – and populate various media with them.

5. Launch Your Grassroots Program

You'd lose all gained momentum if your grassroots advocates register for your program and then wait a year to take their first social action. Roll out your program only when there's an issue that requires action, preferably one most people already know and doesn't need much teaching to execute.

For instance, your first call-to-action could ask advocates to write on various media to elected officials and other influential people in your state about the challenges you observed – and seek to alleviate them.

As your grassroots advocacy program scales up, consider inviting affiliates in your local community or state to join you in subsequent actions in your advocacy program.

6. Don't Stop Recruiting Advocates

Don't stop recruiting advocates. It can also help to inspire others to take on ambassadorial roles by talking to others about your initiatives, sharing social media campaigns, or encouraging many people to sign up as advocates. One way to incentivize recruitment is to link it to some game or competition that offers a reward system to winners.

An effective way to recruit and retain your advocates is by giving credit to your ambassadors when your team wins or receives public recognition for its efforts. This recognition boosts their morale, enhances rapport, and increases their trust in your team, further encouraging their continued engagement in the association.

Measuring and Amplifying Your Impacts

Whether you create a nonprofit, become a social entrepreneur, launch a for-profit business venture, or pursue some other skill or profession, you're working toward advocating your brand.

That's because you're working to *sell* yourself (or an idea) to an audience, a client, or a community.

An effective brand advocacy would generate credibility and authenticity for your brand. It can also raise brand awareness, increase customer trust, and help you convert more customers.

However, like with every other form of marketing, understanding how to measure your impact is critical for success. Meanwhile, data from your impact measurements can help show you what you'll require to amplify your impact and reach a wider audience.

Here are some helpful ways to measure your advocacy program and enhance its impact.

1. Analyze Your Social Media Engagement Metrics

Measuring your social media engagement metrics helps you determine how much of a rave your advocates generate around your brand.

Does the analytics show that people share your content more? Do people comment or like your posts often? What are people saying – not just to you – but about you online?

Where you had to hire influencers to market your brand, it helps to ensure you choose influencers whose profile matches your organization's goals.

Do these influencers have interests that align with your brand? Is their audience willing to hear about your brand's story and cause?

By targeting and leveraging the ideal demographics and interests, you can generate enough engagement and boost your conversion rates.

2. Monitor Feedback from Your Audience

Monitoring customer reviews and feedback is crucial to find out what your audience or beneficiaries think of you and how your program enhances their experience.

A helpful way to do this is to have a repertoire of all feedback you receive from clients, both onsite and online. These could either include first-person comments or social media reviews. Audit all the feedback you've received so far to monitor any changes, improvements, or corrections people offer the brand.

Remember to be proactive here. Don't hesitate to ask your audience to share a testimonial or do a review after you've reached out to or sold a product to them.

Surveys can come in very handy here. You can then use the feedback you garnered to determine aspects of your brand that people like and those you need to improve.

Amplifying Your Social Impact

Once you have the right metrics from customer feedback and technological analytics about your program's performance, you're ready to begin working toward amplifying your impact.

Here are some tips to help you do that.

1. Identify other people or websites with a strong affinity for your brand and suggest they join your advocacy program – or lend a voice to it.

2. Ensure to transmit your brand's missions, values, and identity in all communications, from social media handles to your blogs and hand-outs. This can help enforce the human side of your brand and further impress your brand on your audience.

3. Highlight success stories and testimonials from people who enjoyed your services.

4. Engage in targeted marketing campaigns on sites like Facebook, Instagram, or Google Ads.

5. Develop a strategy to follow up with clients and beneficiaries. That way, you can connect with them more personally and possibly win their confidence or retain their patronage.

Finally, never forget that brand advocacy won't happen overnight. It's a long-term strategy that requires patience, diligence, and employing the right information.

However, rather than allow the long-term wait to scare you from taking action, concentrate on improving your current audience and team's experiences. With time, your brand will build on itself.

Workbook 9

Create a 3-month plan to contribute positively to your community. If possible, get along with some friends on the challenge.

Review your (or your team's) performance after three months. Celebrate your victories, correct your shortcomings, and get set for another series of brand advocacy programs.

Takeaway 9

As you grow in business and impact, you'll quickly learn that people often care less about what you know or even have until they're sure you *care*.

Remember, you'll always need existing technologies to deliver new or innovative tech solutions.

Never run advocacy programs without a plan to measure your efforts. And when the metrics assess your efforts, apply lessons learned to amplify your impacts.

In all you do, stay ethical and use approaches that don't harm or hurt others.

Conclusion

As your final workbook must have suggested to you, the journey to creating a successful career that impacts your life and your world never ends – even in your teens.

And just like running a successful startup, writing this book has been an emotional journey for me, too – for various reasons.

First, the book is reminiscent of various financial and career tips that helped me while I was in my teens, plus those that took me years beyond my teen years to stumble on.

Second, I CAN'T WAIT to read amazing feedback and wholesome reviews from you or a teen reader you purchased this book for. I can't wait to hear how this easy-to-use self-help manual has helped to shape and reshape the reader's perspectives on effective career planning without a college degree.

In the first part, I showed you how to separate your passion from hobbies and only pursue career paths that match your unique strengths. From there, I encouraged you to break out from societal expectations (if or when necessary) to explore Non-Traditional career paths, highlighting several inspiring stories from industry leaders.

I also explained the importance of setting SMART career goals that match your interests, passions, and goals in the second chapter. Of course, you only increase your earning potential as you increase your skill set and professional experience. That's why I outlined the smartest way to gain helpful internships, apprenticeships, networks, and courses that take you from where you are to where your career path points.

The second part dives deeper into the career world by showing you how to craft standout resumes, CVs, and portfolios that make your brand stand out in the job market. And once the finances start turning in? It's time to apply time-tested financial management wisdoms that show you how to budget smartly, understand credit, invest profitably, and save for a rainy day.

Suppose you needed profitable business ideas to try your hands on or where to get the right funds to finance your idea. I'm sure the fifth chapter must have set you on course by pointing out many side hustle ideas and where to get funding to get your brand running.

Next, I showed you helpful tips that have helped many successful remote work teams and leaders thrive. Remote work or not, every teen brand owner needs the right entrepreneurial mindset throughout their career journey.

The right entrepreneurial mindset helps you assess your resources, identify business opportunities, and create a successful business plan to match. It also enables you to market your brand to the right audience, manage your cash flow, and navigate legalities while embracing failures as opportunities to iterate.

In the third and final part, I explored how your personal development is crucial to your all-round career success, as is making a positive social impact on the world around you.

You've learned that even the biggest names in Wall Street may have as much self-doubt as you do, but treating criticism and rejection correctly has helped many of them remain in their industry's creme de la creme. Lastly, regardless of your industry, showing empathy to people and your environment can amplify your positive impact and boost your brand's image as a socially conscious enterprise.

I drop my pen from this end and anticipate yours to bleed in the active application of the principles I've shared in this book – and in sharing the amazing testimonies about how impactful my little gift has been,

I leave you with the very words with which I launched this book's first part:

See you AT THE VERY TOP!!!!

Of course, I won't hesitate to invite you to share your comments, reviews, and suggestions on this material on Amazon (where you purchased it). It's a way to help other teens and teen educators or parents enjoy the same things you've learned in this book.

It'll also encourage me and my team to keep an eye on young people and their career progress and possibly create helpful materials to drive home time-tested life and career principles for lasting success.

THANK YOU SO MUCH FOR TAKING THE TIME TO EXPLORE MY BOOK!

My earnest wish is that you've discovered meaningful insights within these pages.

It truly means the world to me that from all the books out there in this topic, you chose to pick up my book. Once again, thank you.

While you're here, I just want to ask something...

Can I borrow a minute of your time and ask you to leave me an honest feedback on Amazon?

Or a star-rating would be much appreciated. It will only two clicks to leave a rating.

Once again, thank you for being part of my journey and thank you in advance for your thoughtful contribution.

SCAN THIS CODE TO LEAVE A RATING ON AMAZON.COM

References

Academy of Mine (2023)

5 Benefits of Self-Paced Learning

https://www.google.com/url?sa=t&source=web&rct=j&opi=89978449&url=https://w
ww.academyofmine.com/self-paced-learning-benefits/&ved=2ahUKEwiPkNSO_L-
AAxWTiFwKHfjRD9UQFnoECC4QAQ&usg=AOvVaw2KF4Bxnx6l8qKlIFDTtaSF

Adams, R.L. (2016)

10 Rules for Leveraging Social Media to Grow Your Business

https://www.google.com/url?sa=t&source=web&rct=j&opi=89978449&url=https://w
ww.entrepreneur.com/science-technology/10-rules-for-leveraging-social-media-
to-grow-your-
business/284918&ved=2ahUKEwjSqLuog8CAAxVDh1wKHavNAGAQFnoECDIQAQ
&usg=AOvVaw1j0rSbQSJf3wdX0wSyMl4g

AIContentfy Team (2023)

Navigating Legal Issues for Startups

https://www.google.com/url?sa=t&source=web&rct=j&opi=89978449&url=https://ai
contentfy.com/en/blog/navigating-legal-issues-for-
startups%3Fhs_amp%3Dtrue&ved=2ahUKEwiAiOL6iMCAAxVXUkEAHRAwDdkQF
noECAwQAQ&usg=AOvVaw3zmN-BiL-1Uru8dRUHY_G2

Allanah Faherty (Retrieved September 2023)

15 of the Best Remote Jobs to Pursue in 2023

https://www.google.com/url?sa=t&source=web&rct=j&opi=89978449&url=https://w
ww.oberlo.com/blog/best-remote-jobs&ved=2ahUKEwjmks7n-b-
AAxWUW0EAHcylCMsQFnoECAwQBQ&usg=AOvVaw1Ne6oj3AXFb6jTVvXZQrY7

Bank of America (Retrieved September 2023)

Creating a Budget

https://www.google.com/url?sa=t&source=web&rct=j&opi=89978449&url=https://b
ettermoneyhabits.bankofamerica.com/en/saving-budgeting/creating-a-
budget&ved=2ahUKEwjjhKzAg8CAAxXCnFwKHYwGBEoQFnoECAwQBQ&usg=AO
vVaw0izv_QhY8Gv6PKziV32o4V

Becca (2023)

How to Get a Remote Job in 2023

https://www.google.com/url?sa=t&source=web&rct=j&opi=89978449&url=https://w
ww.halfhalftravel.com/remote-work/how-to-get-a-remote-
job.html&ved=2ahUKEwjmks7n-b-
AAxWUW0EAHcyICMsQFnoECCUQAQ&usg=AOvVaw0rc3s1671jkLa9matSkPtv

Beckman, K (2023)

Interviewing 101: How to Navigate the Process from Start to Finish

https://www.google.com/url?sa=t&source=web&rct=j&opi=89978449&url=https://ri
pplematch.com/career-advice/interviewing-101-how-to-navigate-the-process-
from-start-to-finish-
edca38ca/&ved=2ahUKEwiZ_t3egsCAAxUkXEEAHaNcADcQFnoECBwQAQ&usg=A
OvVaw1ENkVerXmDDNQQqpnX1Dpg

Being the Boss (Retrieved September 2023)

How to Take Rejection and Criticism Like a Champ

https://www.google.com/url?sa=t&source=web&rct=j&opi=89978449&url=https://e
quitablemoneyproject.com/2018/11/how-to-handle-rejection-and-criticism-like-a-
champ/&ved=2ahUKEwjL2KPSicCAAxXjQkEAHT9fA00QFnoECCEQAQ&usg=AOvV
aw0xqyuOvle9NvHVtUW1mreY

Bennett, K (2023)

How to Start and Build an Emergency Fund

https://www.google.com/url?sa=t&source=web&rct=j&opi=89978449&url=https://w
ww.bankrate.com/banking/savings/starting-an-emergency-
fund/%23:~:text%3DAn%2520emergency%2520fund%2520should%2520cover,o
n%2520your%2520income%2520and%2520expenses.&ved=2ahUKEwj4uqalhMC
AAxUtWEEAHRvrBOwQFnoECBIQBQ&usg=AOvVaw0PJanTNVQG3qxVV4HHRLhU

Bernard Marr & Co. (Retrieved September 2023)

The Biggest Benefits of the Gig Economy for Freelancers and Businesses

References

https://www.google.com/url?sa=t&source=web&rct=j&opi=89978449&url=https://bernardmarr.com/the-biggest-benefits-of-the-gig-economy-for-freelancers-and-businesses/&ved=2ahUKEwib1e2Fg8CAAxW1RkEAHeBpD80QFnoECCgQAQ&usg=AOvVaw2nTU-d8tovU0adtEB0ayz4

Blair, L (Retrieved September 2023)

Use Surveys to Measure and Amplify Impact

https://www.google.com/url?sa=t&source=web&rct=j&opi=89978449&url=https://apply.surveymonkey.com/resources/use-surveys-to-measure-and-amplify-impact/&ved=2ahUKEwjlq5WSi8CAAxVbiVwKHRFRCxcQFnoECCQQAQ&usg=AOvVaw0ofly7MEimXvbmFGsyXEF6

Bouchrika, I. (2023)

10 Best Open-Source Learning Management Systems (LMS) in 2023

https://www.google.com/url?sa=t&source=web&rct=j&opi=89978449&url=https://research.com/software/best-open-source-learning-management-systems&ved=2ahUKEwio1f_o_L-AAxV3UUEAHYiRBlgQFnoECA0QAQ&usg=AOvVaw2adlp4YS4rQiu0AXNkVSqn

Brown, A (2022)

Implementing Effective Mentorship in Apprenticeships: Best Practices for Employers and Intermediaries

https://www.google.com/url?sa=t&source=web&rct=j&opi=89978449&url=https://www.apprentix.io/post/implementing-effective-mentorship-in-apprenticeships-best-practices-for-employers-and-intermediaries&ved=2ahUKEwjL5Ni--b-AAxXxW0EAHXDzDO0QFnoECC0QAQ&usg=AOvVaw3Vl7gGZu69yQBeaYjLCQpS

Brook, C. (2022)

5 Key Ways to Develop and Entrepreneurial Mindset

https://www.google.com/url?sa=t&source=web&rct=j&opi=89978449&url=https://www.businessbecause.com/news/entrepreneurs/8279/how-to-develop-an-entrepreneurial-mindset%3Fsponsored&ved=2ahUKEwjLk4qhiMCAAxWMW0EAHW0-DQoQFnoECA0QBQ&usg=AOvVaw0KzymUmp8bM5tB7rITKzYj

Caramels, S (2023)

Tips for Making a Great Resume

https://www.google.com/url?sa=t&source=web&rct=j&opi=89978449&url=https://www.businessnewsdaily.com/3207-resume-writing-

tips.html&ved=2ahUKEwi7vvjTgcCAAxVRQEEAHWeQAX0QFnoECCgQAQ&usg=A
OvVaw0ZcMF2sHsq-E5OleE7pW-k

Careers in Public Health. (Retrieved September 2023)

How to Build and Develop Your Network by Using Social Media

https://www.google.com/url?sa=t&source=web&rct=j&opi=89978449&url=https://w
ww.careersinpublichealth.net/resources/how-build-develop-your-network-by-
using-social-media/&ved=2ahUKEwj23djp-r-
AAxWiQkEAHbOEB6cQFnoECC0QAQ&usg=AOvVaw2F_KKhZt9UZbEPQRHHuJpX

Carpenter, A (2023)

How to Use Online Learning Platforms to Develop Technical Skills

https://www.google.com/url?sa=t&source=web&rct=j&opi=89978449&url=https://w
ww.softwareadvice.com/resources/online-learning-
platforms/&ved=2ahUKEwjy86n6-b-
AAxXKXUEAHdETDrUQFnoECBYQAQ&usg=AOvVaw2HqCzBgU1gFMK8kX1-
bWxR

Capital Placements (2022)

The Importance of Internships: Top 5 Reasons Why Internships Are Critical

https://www.google.com/url?sa=t&source=web&rct=j&opi=89978449&url=https://c
apital-placement.com/blog/the-importance-of-an-internship-top-5-reasons-why-
internships-are-critical/&ved=2ahUKEwjpq_mV_r-
AAxWGR8AKHSKICpEQFnoECCEQAQ&usg=AOvVaw3lhxJOMI08w9Ohf83NFY2E

Chen, J (2023)

Debt: What It Is, How It Works, Types, and Ways to Pay Back

https://www.google.com/url?sa=t&source=web&rct=j&opi=89978449&url=https://w
ww.investopedia.com/terms/d/debt.asp&ved=2ahUKEwjYq9Lhg8CAAxVdQUEAH
d8hDHUQFnoECB8QAQ&usg=AOvVaw2uCHEJw_D1z6gP-f6JrD-4

Chen, J (2023)

Long Term: Definition in Investing for Companies and Individual

https://www.google.com/url?sa=t&source=web&rct=j&opi=89978449&url=https://w
ww.investopedia.com/terms/l/longterm.asp&ved=2ahUKEwiP5MHwg8CAAxV6SO
EAHRJpBlcQFnoECBIQAQ&usg=AOvVaw0581NKMAdT0ssTil-7tywD

Choi, Y. and Sung-in Chang (2023)

A Study of the Influence of Civic Engagement in the Relationship between
Psychological Capital and Social Performance

References

https://www.google.com/url?sa=t&source=web&rct=j&opi=89978449&url=https://www.tandfonline.com/doi/full/10.1080/23311975.2023.2195643&ved=2ahUKEwjMor-7isCAAxURQ8AKHTOFBXoQFnoECCsQAQ&usg=AOvVaw36HWRzmeguhfIT7dBasgon

Clear, J (Retrieved September 2023)

Goal-Setting: A Scientific Guide to Setting and Achieving Goals

https://www.google.com/url?sa=t&source=web&rct=j&opi=89978449&url=https://jamesclear.com/goal-setting&ved=2ahUKEwio8Lue-L-AAxW2XEEAHZsbBT0QFnoECGYQAQ&usg=AOvVaw2OzN-Ibe_ERtIkfSU0Tk2S

Clennon, R (2023)

Startup Secrets to Leveraging Open-Source Software

https://www.google.com/url?sa=t&source=web&rct=j&opi=89978449&url=https://www.linkedin.com/pulse/startup-secrets-leveraging-open-source-software-romeo-clennon&ved=2ahUKEwio1f_o_L-AAxV3UUEAHYiRBlgQjjh6BAgQEAE&usg=AOvVaw3oo3i6-Xift7toM2LpWisU

Cote, C. (2022)

How to Identify Business and Market Opportunities

https://www.google.com/url?sa=t&source=web&rct=j&opi=89978449&url=https://online.hbs.edu/blog/post/how-to-identify-business-opportunities&ved=2ahUKEwjx_pKxiMCAAxVSe8AKHQ-jCX4QFnoECBkQAQ&usg=AOvVaw0TH_A_COBWByqXoS045xN_

Coursera (2023)

21 Side Hustles and How to Get Started

https://www.google.com/url?sa=t&source=web&rct=j&opi=89978449&url=https://www.coursera.org/articles/side-hustle&ved=2ahUKEwiLq4umhMCAAxXIWkEAHZ3PCyEQFnoECD0QAQ&usg=AOvVaw3aFkIvO0sq7bF-APtdI-JH

Coursera (2023)

Technology Skills: What They Are and How to Improve Them

https://www.google.com/url?sa=t&source=web&rct=j&opi=89978449&url=https://www.coursera.org/articles/technology-skills&ved=2ahUKEwjnoIP-_L-AAxUNW0EAHQIgCnEQFnoECCsQAQ&usg=AOvVaw0NVJ6mQ0xIP-Ba09jcpzYw

Coursera (2023)

Transferable Skills: How to Use Them to Land Your Next Job

https://www.google.com/url?sa=t&source=web&rct=j&opi=89978449&url=https://www.coursera.org/articles/transferable-skills&ved=2ahUKEwiDwdai_L-AAxW8UUEAHcxPC8oQFnoECCUQAQ&usg=AOvVaw2MLKm7PFz5X-cc-NRax6BP

Cox, L.K. (2023)

Imposter Syndrome: 8 Ways to Deal with It before It Hinders Your Success

https://www.google.com/url?sa=t&source=web&rct=j&opi=89978449&url=https://blog.hubspot.com/marketing/impostor-syndrome-tips&ved=2ahUKEwiZiurFicCAAxUFR8AKHXBDCV0QFnoECCYQAQ&usg=AOvVaw0gBcjIMB86FxX2kgNnyRMG

Dessau, L. (2005)

10 Tools for Dealing with Criticism and Rejection

https://www.google.com/url?sa=t&source=web&rct=j&opi=89978449&url=https://talentdevelop.com/articles/10ToolsFD.html&ved=2ahUKEwjL2KPSicCAAxXjQkEAHT9fA00QFnoECBYQBQ&usg=AOvVaw2X43WgfkVSQO6H2Ux3DFee

Digital Learning Software (Retrieved September 2023)

What Is Self-Paced Learning: Definition, Benefits, and Tips

https://www.google.com/url?sa=t&source=web&rct=j&opi=89978449&url=https://www.digitallearninginstitute.com/what-is-self-paced-learning-definition-benefits-and-tips/&ved=2ahUKEwiPkNS0_L-AAxWTiFwKHfjRD9UQFnoECDQQAQ&usg=AOvVaw1ZvUJymLDMrl0ERvAtAT_n

Discover Praxis (Retrieved September 2023)

Don't Go to College for the Social Experience (How to Network without College)

https://www.google.com/url?sa=t&source=web&rct=j&opi=89978449&url=https://discoverpraxis.com/blog/11387/dont-try-build-college-network%3Fhs_amp%3Dtrue&ved=2ahUKEwj23djp-r-AAxWiQkEAHbOEB6cQFnoECA8QAQ&usg=AOvVaw1Xtc8-MdRhK-jqyZAYCYxG

DO-IT (Retrieved September 2023)

How Do I Develop a Support Network?

https://www.google.com/url?sa=t&source=web&rct=j&opi=89978449&url=https://www.washington.edu/doit/how-can-i-develop-support-network%23:~:text%3DAttend%2520events%2520that%2520put%2520you,help%2520you%2520reach%2520your%2520goals.&ved=2ahUKEwizx7bhicCAAxVJFcAKHY27BaUQFnoECBMQBQ&usg=AOvVaw3_Uc7z0N_wrxVPkkrTaCLq

References

Dukes, B. (Retrieved September 2023)

Beyond Venture Capital: Exploring Funding Options for Entrepreneurs in 2023

https://www.google.com/url?sa=t&source=web&rct=j&opi=89978449&url=https://e
xitwise.com/blog/beyond-venture-capital-exploring-funding-options-for-
entrepreneurs-in-
2023&ved=2ahUKEwizq_K3hMCAAxUFR8AKHXBDCV0QFnoECDIQAQ&usg=AOv
Vaw07gyMoCb51IYTUhttstpgL

Eads, A (2023)

15 Ways to Find Your Passion in Life

https://www.google.com/url?sa=t&source=web&rct=j&opi=89978449&url=https://w
ww.indeed.com/career-advice/finding-a-job/how-to-find-your-
passion&ved=2ahUKEwj8_vGd9r-
AAxWzRkEAHc3kAmQQFnoECA4QAQ&usg=AOvVaw0Uizw0UZujBaePXNqV8DhU

Eads, A (2023)

35 of the Best Remote Jobs to Pursue (with BLS Outlook)

https://www.google.com/url?sa=t&source=web&rct=j&opi=89978449&url=https://w
ww.indeed.com/career-advice/finding-a-job/best-remote-
jobs&ved=2ahUKEwjmks7n-b-
AAxWUW0EAHcyICMsQFnoECBIQAQ&usg=AOvVaw3b0FOetZgm_h7vhQYnCVzQ

Editorial (Dosomething.org)

73 Community Service Project Ideas

https://www.google.com/url?sa=t&source=web&rct=j&opi=89978449&url=https://w
ww.dosomething.org/us/articles/community-service-project-
ideas&ved=2ahUKEwjijP3eisCAAxXZRkEAHZyBBGcQFnoECBMQBQ&usg=AOvVa
w0PRQ8675SuuA_qS1YliPCb

Enterprise League (2021)

5 Tips for Creating Boundaries between Work and Personal Life

https://www.google.com/url?sa=t&source=web&rct=j&opi=89978449&url=https://e
nterpriseleague.com/blog/boundaries-between-work-and-personal-
life/&ved=2ahUKEwjd9_Wzh8CAAxWHLcAKHVyvARMQFnoECCkQAQ&usg=AOvV
aw1EpTt8uwHq9mOJ7oLCpLDR

Epstein, J. and Yuthas, K (2017)

Amplifying Your Impact

https://www.google.com/url?sa=t&source=web&rct=j&opi=89978449&url=https://www.researchgate.net/publication/331747387_Amplifying_Your_Impact&ved=2ahUKEwjlq5WSi8CAAxVbiVwKHRFRCxcQFnoECCgQAQ&usg=AOvVaw2nSli57iszgeZJ9x00TJIK

Eruteya, K (2023)

You're Not an Imposter. You're Actually Pretty Amazing

https://www.google.com/url?sa=t&source=web&rct=j&opi=89978449&url=https://hbr.org/2022/01/youre-not-an-imposter-youre-actually-pretty-amazing&ved=2ahUKEwiZiurFicCAAxUFR8AKHXBDCV0QFnoECCEQAQ&usg=AOvVaw3OhJ3e_hKlVmMtOtkS5xt8

Every Woman (Retrieved September 2023)

Understanding Your Strengths in 9 Simple Steps

https://www.google.com/url?sa=t&source=web&rct=j&opi=89978449&url=https://www.everywoman.com/my-development/understanding-your-strengths-9-simple-steps/&ved=2ahUKEwizwl6t9r-AAxUFBMAKHSUECzsQFnoECBIQBQ&usg=AOvVaw1li_mNKMcDVyU6PFgcSCZn

EU Business School (2022)

How to identify Business Opportunities in Any Market

https://www.google.com/url?sa=t&source=web&rct=j&opi=89978449&url=https://www.euruni.edu/blog/how-to-identify-business-opportunities-in-any-market/&ved=2ahUKEwjx_pKxiMCAAxVSe8AKHQ-jCX4QFnoECB4QBQ&usg=AOvVaw0PabOUzW-boDJixXteg6WM

EY Netherlands (2020)

Thirteen Sources of Finance for Entrepreneurs: Make Sure You Pick the Right

https://www.google.com/url?sa=t&source=web&rct=j&opi=89978449&url=https://www.ey.com/en_nl/finance-navigator/12-sources-of-finance-for-entrepreneurs-make-sure-you-pick-the-right-one&ved=2ahUKEwizq_K3hMCAAxUFR8AKHXBDCV0QFnoECA8QAQ&usg=AOvVaw3gatc338nqA3Y1iFFZPfJl

Federman, B (2021)

Welcome to the New Normal: Seven Ways to Improve Your Adaptability in an Ever-Changing World

https://www.google.com/url?sa=t&source=web&rct=j&opi=89978449&url=https://www.forbes.com/sites/forbescoachescouncil/2021/07/08/welcome-to-the-new-normal-seven-ways-to-improve-your-adaptability-in-an-ever-changing-

world/%3Fsh%3D24a4f8967fb8&ved=2ahUKEwinj7L-hMCAAxXFV0EAHSVHDsYQFnoECEUQAQ&usg=AOvVaw0zVyyNYu-mfoXNjWC4sdiO

Ferguson, E. (2023)

25 Side Hustles: Ideas for Making Money I'm Your Spare Time

https://www.google.com/url?sa=t&source=web&rct=j&opi=89978449&url=https://www.shopify.com/ng/blog/side-hustle&ved=2ahUKEwiLq4umhMCAAxXIWkEAHZ3PCyEQFnoECCoQAQ&usg=AOvVaw1qYBJISxB_0p2SxjukHQO9

Forbes Business Council (2023)

15 Ways Technology Can Drive Innovation and Improve Your Offerings

https://www.google.com/url?sa=t&source=web&rct=j&opi=89978449&url=https://www.forbes.com/sites/forbesbusinesscouncil/2023/04/10/15-ways-technology-can-drive-innovation-and-improve-your-offerings/amp/&ved=2ahUKEwjl76i8hsCAAxXLYcAKHVdBBqsQFnoECCkQAQ&usg=AOvVaw1S5G92YnbloU_RzXtErSui

Forbes Coaching Council (2021)

16 Ways to Set Better Work-Life Balance by Setting Better Boundaries

https://www.google.com/url?sa=t&source=web&rct=j&opi=89978449&url=https://www.forbes.com/sites/forbescoachescouncil/2021/02/01/16-ways-to-achieve-work-life-balance-by-setting-better-boundaries/%3Fsh%3D24a1e4964536&ved=2ahUKEwjd9_Wzh8CAAxWHLcAKHVyvARMQFnoECBsQAQ&usg=AOvVaw11wSsUP5UJjlWcRmxXYqIN

Forbes Council Post (2021)

14 Critical Career Skills to Cultivate in the Digital Era

https://www.google.com/url?sa=t&source=web&rct=j&opi=89978449&url=https://www.forbes.com/sites/forbesbusinesscouncil/2021/12/08/14-critical-career-skills-to-cultivate-in-the-digital-era/amp/&ved=2ahUKEwjnoIP-_L-AAxUNW0EAHQIgCnEQFnoECDAQAQ&usg=AOvVaw1W04MOZ0L1p4VON5uDwJj8

Freedman, M (2023)

How to Write a Self-Assessment: 5 Tips to Improve Your Evaluation

https://www.google.com/url?sa=t&source=web&rct=j&opi=89978449&url=https://www.businessnewsdaily.com/5379-writing-self-

assessment.html&ved=2ahUKEwi1zNOL-L-
AAxVYWUEAHXtMDmIQFnoECDwQAQ&usg=AOvVaw1RbK4AqTasjhQFQ6PFegT3

Gallant, C (2021)

4 Steps to Building a Profitable Portfolio

https://www.google.com/url?sa=t&source=web&rct=j&opi=89978449&url=https://w
ww.investopedia.com/financial-advisor/steps-building-profitable-
portfolio/&ved=2ahUKEwinhLnugsCAAxXKEsAKHbHbC8AQFnoECEMQAQ&usg=A
OvVaw3jTzKGIHL4O7dtCqRFmjz7

Garibay, C (2023)

8 Stories of Successful Entrepreneurs That Will Inspire You On Your Journey

https://www.google.com/url?sa=t&source=web&rct=j&opi=89978449&url=https://v
aliantceo.com/stories-of-successful-entrepreneurs/&ved=2ahUKEwjPlrHx97-
AAxXWTkEAHZ--D68QFnoECCIQAQ&usg=AOvVaw1_CtDi-6aKxSEILqf5s6ZF

Georgiadis, C. (2022)

How to Brand Yourself as an Entrepreneur in 7 Steps

https://www.google.com/url?sa=t&source=web&rct=j&opi=89978449&url=https://w
ww.forbes.com/sites/theyec/2022/11/09/how-to-brand-yourself-as-an-
entrepreneur-in-7-
steps/amp/&ved=2ahUKEwj1vLXQiMCAAxWPSUEAHVnpD70QFnoECA8QAQ&usg
=AOvVaw1NqdccbaTaLkIztz66iWlv

GFOA (2022)

10 Steps to Long-Term Financial Planning

https://www.google.com/url?sa=t&source=web&rct=j&opi=89978449&url=https://w
ww.gfoa.org/materials/gfr422-
10steps&ved=2ahUKEwjki8jWhMCAAxXOTEEAHZYkDXgQFnoECB4QAQ&usg=AO
vVaw1Fc2Mf-iopEBhHOf1Etzpl

GFOA (2022)

Long-Term Financial Planning

https://www.google.com/url?sa=t&source=web&rct=j&opi=89978449&url=https://w
ww.gfoa.org/materials/long-term-financial-
planning&ved=2ahUKEwjki8jWhMCAAxXOTEEAHZYkDXgQFnoECBsQAQ&usg=A
OvVaw29glCRUm-dhL6BQCFkO76b

GRIN (Retrieved September 2023)

10 Ways to Leverage Social Media for Your Business

References

https://www.google.com/url?sa=t&source=web&rct=j&opi=89978449&url=https://g
rin.co/blog/ways-to-leverage-social-media-for-your-
business/&ved=2ahUKEwjSqLuog8CAAxVDh1wKHavNAGAQFnoECBwQBQ&usg=
AOvVaw2Mi4zTyxj2kfUpmENGHHDI

Harvard University (Retrieved September 2023)

Harvard University: Remote Work Revolution for Everyone

https://www.google.com/url?sa=t&source=web&rct=j&opi=89978449&url=https://w
ww.edx.org/course/remote-
work&ved=2ahUKEwiKx4bnhsCAAxUpQEEAHaROBQ4QFnoECDEQAQ&usg=AOvV
aw1xDEuKAXO4SAlj9sGXP69m

Harvard Business School (2022)

4 Entrepreneur Success Stories to Learn From

https://www.google.com/url?sa=t&source=web&rct=j&opi=89978449&url=https://o
nline.hbs.edu/blog/post/successful-entrepreneur-stories&ved=2ahUKEwjPlrHx97

Hayes, A. (2023)

Social Entrepreneur: Definition and Examples

https://www.google.com/url?sa=t&source=web&rct=j&opi=89978449&url=https://w
ww.investopedia.com/terms/s/social-entrepreneur.asp&ved=2ahUKEwjMor-
7isCAAxURQ8AKHTOFBXoQFnoECCkQAQ&usg=AOvVaw0J9csDGS_1JxSSXXXy
HKys

Heaven, C. (Retrieved September 2023)

Developing a Plan for Assessing Local Needs and Resources

https://www.google.com/url?sa=t&source=web&rct=j&opi=89978449&url=https://ct
b.ku.edu/en/table-of-contents/assessment/assessing-community-needs-and-
resources/develop-a-
plan/main&ved=2ahUKEwj3zeeXicCAAxX_U0EAHblZDpsQFnoECCgQAQ&usg=AO
vVaw3aTy7Vsx9F8bdiWdArkQIM

Herring, B.B. (Retrieved September 2023)

How to Show Remote Work Experience on Your Resume

https://www.google.com/url?sa=t&source=web&rct=j&opi=89978449&url=https://w
ww.flexjobs.com/blog/post/show-remote-work-experience-resume-
v2/&ved=2ahUKEwiUsdPPh8CAAxWeTEEAHfaDDwQQFnoECBoQAQ&usg=AOvVa
w1Pu3GHbNCV3IAR2Q_LsB9j

Herrity, J (2023)

Transferable Skills: 10 Skills that Work Across Industries

https://www.google.com/url?sa=t&source=web&rct=j&opi=89978449&url=https://www.indeed.com/career-advice/resumes-cover-letters/transferable-skills%23:~:text%3DTransferable%2520skills%2520are%2520proficiencies%2520that,candidates%2520with%2520strong%2520communication%2520skills%2520.&ved=2ahUKEwiDwdai_L-AAxW8UUEAHcxPC8oQFnoECA8QBQ&usg=AOvVaw2eXJW8irVTBnqC_O49Uz9D

Herrity, J (2022)

How to Perform a Self-Assessment

https://www.google.com/url?sa=t&source=web&rct=j&opi=89978449&url=https://www.indeed.com/career-advice/career-development/self-assessments&ved=2ahUKEwi1zNOL-L-AAxVYWUEAHXtMDmIQFnoECEAQAQ&usg=AOvVaw3piak2m2N0GFSVce6STgwP

Hiles, C. (2023)

How to Start a Side Hustle

https://www.google.com/url?sa=t&source=web&rct=j&opi=89978449&url=https://time.com/personal-finance/article/start-a-side-hustle/&ved=2ahUKEwiLq4umhMCAAxXIWkEAHZ3PCyEQFnoECBEQBQ&usg=AOvVaw1z8L4akVvHAHjBVDFuM06A

Howington, J. (Retrieved September 2023)

7 Things Employers Look for When Hiring Remote Workers

https://www.google.com/url?sa=t&source=web&rct=j&opi=89978449&url=https://www.flexjobs.com/blog/post/employers-look-hiring-remote-workers/&ved=2ahUKEwiUsdPPh8CAAxWeTEEAHfaDDwQQFnoECBwQAQ&usg=AOvVaw3GM1s3Urh74fRWzb6SAkrb

Huthwaite Internal (2021)

Ten Tips for Effective Virtual Communication

https://www.google.com/url?sa=t&source=web&rct=j&opi=89978449&url=https://www.huthwaiteinternational.com/blog/effective-virtual-communication%3Fhs_amp%3Dtrue&ved=2ahUKEwiAwfiNh8CAAxULR8AKHc2PDHkQFnoECBEQBQ&usg=AOvVaw1NaE1QeIdkHQUFoj0JwHJG

Ideas (Retrieved September 2023)

Remote Work Revolution: Current Opportunities and Challenges for Organizations

References

https://www.google.com/url?sa=t&source=web&rct=j&opi=89978449&url=https://id eas.repec.org/a/ovi/oviste/vxxy2020i1p468-472.html&ved=2ahUKEwiKx4bnhsCAAxUpQEEAHaROBQ4QFnoECDAQAQ&usg=A OvVaw3X40C2IYtJbXxxF7FA9zLW

Indeed Editorial Team (2022)

Important Benefits of Gaining Experience from an Internship

https://www.google.com/url?sa=t&source=web&rct=j&opi=89978449&url=https://c a.indeed.com/career-advice/career-development/experience-from-internship&ved=2ahUKEwjpq_mV_r-AAxWGR8AKHSKICpEQFnoECEMQAQ&usg=AOvVaw1ofSk6CV_JXF-QbW_RXqR_

Indeed Editorial Team (2022)

How to Identify Your Key Strengths in the Workplace

https://www.google.com/url?sa=t&source=web&rct=j&opi=89978449&url=https://w ww.indeed.com/career-advice/career-development/identifying-strengths&ved=2ahUKEwizwl6t9r-AAxUFBMAKHSUECzsQFnoECCcQAQ&usg=AOvVaw2KxU6r7tIW5RwUcORLq38Z

Indeed (2023)

How to Make a Portfolio: A Step-by-Step Guide

https://www.google.com/url?sa=t&source=web&rct=j&opi=89978449&url=https://in .indeed.com/career-advice/career-development/how-to-make-portfolio&ved=2ahUKEwinhLnugsCAAxXKEsAKHbHbC8AQFnoECBoQAQ&usg=A OvVaw2TpddAm-vrE48ISDiWBgOW

Indeed Editorial Team (2023)

Top 8 Effective Tips to Make Your Resume Stand Out

https://www.google.com/url?sa=t&source=web&rct=j&opi=89978449&url=https://w ww.indeed.com/career-advice/resumes-cover-letters/tips-to-make-your-resume-stand-out&ved=2ahUKEwi7vvjTgcCAAxVRQEEAHWeQAX0QFnoECBoQBQ&usg=AOvVa w3T9RpFAYBJKhAJbwAea7uN

Indeed Editorial Team (2023)

How to Improve Your Soft Skills (Plus Their Importance)

https://www.google.com/url?sa=t&source=web&rct=j&opi=89978449&url=https://w ww.indeed.com/career-advice/career-development/how-to-improve-soft-skills&ved=2ahUKEwiB0bPV-7-AAxWZiFwKHX6kBTkQFnoECB0QAQ&usg=AOvVaw0z5wb1XZRyVDJAZpBAa3fd

Indeed Editorial Team (2023)

21 Soft Skills for Leadership Success

https://www.google.com/url?sa=t&source=web&rct=j&opi=89978449&url=https://www.indeed.com/career-advice/career-development/soft-skills-for-leadership&ved=2ahUKEwiB0bPV-7-AAxWZiFwKHX6kBTkQFnoECBwQAQ&usg=AOvVaw3kvwvYN0_nZkfnkyPKsN4G

Indeed Editorial Team (2023)

5 Steps to Create a Career Development Plan for Yourself

https://www.google.com/url?sa=t&source=web&rct=j&opi=89978449&url=https://www.indeed.com/career-advice/career-development/steps-to-create-a-career-development-plan&ved=2ahUKEwiP3-TG-L-AAxVRQEEAHWeQAX0QFnoECBUQAQ&usg=AOvVaw2sSBvWXjjPOoQYtIrzV1Qf

Influencity (2023)

The Power of Brand Advocacy: How to Measure and Amplify Its Impact

https://www.google.com/url?sa=t&source=web&rct=j&opi=89978449&url=https://influencity.com/blog/en/the-power-of-brand-advocacy-how-to-measure-and-amplify-its-impact%3Fhs_amp%3Dtrue&ved=2ahUKEwjlq5WSi8CAAxVbiVwKHRFRCxcQFnoECCoQAQ&usg=AOvVaw32h6PC3r1X6FAcYMApu_da

Investopedia Team (2022)

How to Build an Emergency Fund

https://www.google.com/url?sa=t&source=web&rct=j&opi=89978449&url=https://www.investopedia.com/personal-finance/how-to-build-emergency-fund/&ved=2ahUKEwj4uqalhMCAAxUtWEEAHRvrBOwQFnoECCsQAQ&usg=AOvVaw08nSFG5hnCgKM8q5jrjc1c

Ishi, R (2023)

How to Identify Your Interests and Passions

https://www.google.com/url?sa=t&source=web&rct=j&opi=89978449&url=https://www.caclubindia.com/amp/articles/self-discovery-of-your-interest-and-passion-49380.asp&ved=2ahUKEwj8_vGd9r-AAxWzRkEAHc3kAmQQFnoECBQQBQ&usg=AOvVaw0K1YmwILPj2hGpKqs3OppK

Jesnoewski, A. (2018)

Four Ways to Identify More Business Opportunities

References

https://www.google.com/url?sa=t&source=web&rct=j&opi=89978449&url=https://www.smartcompany.com.au/startupsmart/advice/business-planning/four-ways-to-identify-more-business-opportunities/&ved=2ahUKEwjx_pKxiMCAAxVSe8AKHQ-jCX4QFnoECCkQAQ&usg=AOvVaw3bcMrz8jUT-EzAU5vRauWu

Kane, S (2018)

11 Ways to Cultivate Resilience

https://www.google.com/url?sa=t&source=web&rct=j&opi=89978449&url=https://psychcentral.com/lib/11-ways-to-cultivate-resilience&ved=2ahUKEwiSpfWqicCAAxV6S0EAHRJpBlcQFnoECAsQAQ&usg=AOvVaw1dnMq0Z-YvAkELg5MjxcKJ

Kahless (2023)

The Gig Economy and Freelancing: What's the Catch?

https://www.google.com/url?sa=t&source=web&rct=j&opi=89978449&url=https://capital-placement.com/blog/the-catch-freelancing-and-gig-economy/&ved=2ahUKEwib1e2Fg8CAAxW1RkEAHeBpD80QFnoECBIQAQ&usg=AOvVaw12PhfVScH5XvmRvxLzDA-F

King, M (2023)

The Art of Finding a Job

https://www.google.com/url?sa=t&source=web&rct=j&opi=89978449&url=https://www.forbes.com/sites/forbescoachescouncil/2020/11/18/the-art-of-finding-a-job/%3Fsh%3D24a840961bc8&ved=2ahUKEwjm6sv1gcCAAxV-XUEAHTEqAyQQFnoECB0QAQ&usg=AOvVaw1UPQP7E84YdadfAUyah1XW

Knight, K. and Maher, L. (2022)

How Funders Can Help Fill Critical Gaps in Technology for Social Good

https://www.google.com/url?sa=t&source=web&rct=j&opi=89978449&url=https://givingcompass.org/article/leveraging-technology-for-social-change&ved=2ahUKEwiHjfDOisCAAxXXgVwKHQPyA0cQFnoECCYQAQ&usg=AOvVaw3puHv9hMOn0CyTNaQugXrR

Laundry, L. (2019)

Emotional Intelligence Skills: What They Are and How to Develop Them

https://www.google.com/url?sa=t&source=web&rct=j&opi=89978449&url=https://online.hbs.edu/blog/post/emotional-intelligence-skills&ved=2ahUKEwi6wJy5icCAAxXnXUEAHWkuCTUQFnoECCEQAQ&usg=AOvVaw2u_ARI4JyCZnM4G7Y0--t3

Leonardus, N. and Brian, F. (2023)

27 Best Online Collaboration Tools for Productive Teamwork in 2023

https://www.google.com/url?sa=t&source=web&rct=j&opi=89978449&url=https://w
ww.hostinger.com/tutorials/best-online-collaboration-
tools&ved=2ahUKEwjWr9mdh8CAAxXaW0EAHRAQA-
YQFnoECA8QAQ&usg=AOvVaw03jjPQFfg6Xr5D-8JAgGGM

LinkedIn Community (Retrieved September 2023)

How Do You Learn from Failure and Iterate Quickly in Innovation Development?

https://www.google.com/url?sa=t&source=web&rct=j&opi=89978449&url=https://w
ww.linkedin.com/advice/0/how-do-you-learn-from-failure-iterate-
quickly&ved=2ahUKEwjCo9aJicCAAxWcQUEAHc7PAB4QFnoECBMQAQ&usg=AO
vVaw1Ub2duTlSmst3U8GJdm3aH

Law, J.T (2022)

Entrepreneurial Thinking: 20 Ways to Think Like an Entrepreneur

https://www.google.com/url?sa=t&source=web&rct=j&opi=89978449&url=https://w
ww.oberlo.com/blog/entrepreneurial-
mindset&ved=2ahUKEwjLk4qhiMCAAxWMW0EAHW0-
DQoQFnoECBkQAQ&usg=AOvVaw0EX8WMTHJPnU-M_zThrZWl

LinkedIn Community (Retrieved September 2023)

What Are the Most Effective Ways to Leverage Technology for Social Change?

https://www.google.com/url?sa=t&source=web&rct=j&opi=89978449&url=https://w
ww.linkedin.com/advice/1/what-most-effective-ways-leverage-
technology&ved=2ahUKEwiHjfDOisCAAxXXgVwKHQPyA0cQFnoECA4QAQ&usg=
AOvVaw1K52w47lQ3z2vLLcHDm2Hb

LinkedIn Community (Retrieved September 2023)

How Do You Measure and Report the Outcomes and Impacts of Your Research

https://www.google.com/url?sa=t&source=web&rct=j&opi=89978449&url=https://w
ww.linkedin.com/advice/0/how-do-you-measure-report-outcomes-impacts-your-
2e&ved=2ahUKEwjIq5WSi8CAAxVbiVwKHRFRCxcQFnoECBsQAQ&usg=AOvVaw2
22hPv9RMlI_FUsL5KjIQX

Liggy (2022)

How to Embrace Lifelong Learning

References

https://www.google.com/url?sa=t&source=web&rct=j&opi=89978449&url=https://w
ww.liggywebb.com/how-to-embrace-lifelong-learning/&ved=2ahUKEwiw1u3j_b-
AAxV5WEEAHWWjAisQFnoECCkQAQ&usg=AOvVaw2Tq_duYC4hglYobrhwAWRJ

LinkedIn Community (Retrieved September 2023)

How Can You Leverage Your Mentors' Network and Expertise for Your Career
Growth?

https://www.google.com/url?sa=t&source=web&rct=j&opi=89978449&url=https://w
ww.linkedin.com/advice/0/how-can-you-leverage-your-mentors-
network&ved=2ahUKEwjL5Ni--b-
AAxXxW0EAHXDzDO0QFnoECBMQAQ&usg=AOvVaw0GFzcA27TrVhjz6mNlpkoJ

Linn, A. (2023)

How to Build a Social Network

https://www.google.com/url?sa=t&source=web&rct=j&opi=89978449&url=https://w
ww.wikihow.com/Build-a-Social-Network&ved=2ahUKEwj23djp-r-
AAxWiQkEAHbOEB6cQFnoECA4QAQ&usg=AOvVaw38vny5dpF7wY-7sgyu0bZm

Masterclass (2021)

Business 101: How to Develop an Entrepreneurial Mindset

https://www.google.com/url?sa=t&source=web&rct=j&opi=89978449&url=https://w
ww.masterclass.com/articles/how-to-develop-an-entrepreneurial-
mindset&ved=2ahUKEwjLk4qhiMCAAxWMW0EAHW0-
DQoQFnoECDsQAQ&usg=AOvVaw2yWQ2tvjTchFihND9KL9To

Matthew, N (2018)

Tips to Build a Successful Brand/Business for Millennials

https://www.google.com/url?sa=t&source=web&rct=j&opi=89978449&url=https://w
ww.entrepreneur.com/en-in/starting-a-business/brand-building-on-a-serious-
note-for-young-
entrepreneurs/321534&ved=2ahUKEwj1vLXQiMCAAxWPSUEAHVnpD70QFnoEC
A4QAQ&usg=AOvVaw3ofMSaSH__LYHvcsulvO2_

Menjivar, J. (Retrieved September 2023)

10 Volunteering Opportunities in Your Community

https://www.google.com/url?sa=t&source=web&rct=j&opi=89978449&url=https://w
ww.dosomething.org/us/articles/volunteering-opportunities-in-your-
community&ved=2ahUKEwjijP3eisCAAxXZRkEAHZyBBGcQFnoECCQQAQ&usg=A
OvVaw3sij3S6K6ANkFitDuU8aGk

MentorCruise (2023)

Creating a Personalized Career Roadmap for Success

https://www.google.com/url?sa=t&source=web&rct=j&opi=89978449&url=https://www.linkedin.com/pulse/creating-personalized-career-roadmap-success-mentorcruise%3Ftrk%3Dpulse-article_more-articles_related-content-card&ved=2ahUKEwiP3-TG-L-AAxVRQEEAHWeQAX0Qjjh6BAgpEAE&usg=AOvVaw1bLAvVevI93MEccvDXHKQj

MindTools (2018)

Developing Resilience

https://www.google.com/url?sa=t&source=web&rct=j&opi=89978449&url=https://www.mindtools.com/ao310a2/developing-resilience&ved=2ahUKEwiSpfWqicCAAxV6S0EAHRJpBlcQFnoECDwQAQ&usg=AOvVaw37ksVYkLHckeZYBYliwB_X

Money Advice (Retrieved September 2023)

Ways to Stick to Your Budget and Jumpstart Your Savings

https://www.google.com/url?sa=t&source=web&rct=j&opi=89978449&url=https://www.valleyfirst.com/simple-advice/money/ways-to-stick-to-your-budget&ved=2ahUKEwjjhKzAg8CAAxXCnFwKHYwGBEoQFnoECCUQAQ&usg=AOvVaw28A7XsFn-p-uyVwVAKuu3u

Muff K., and Dyllick, T. (2022)

Measuring and Amplifying Impact

https://www.google.com/url?sa=t&source=web&rct=j&opi=89978449&url=https://www.aacsb.edu/insights/articles/2022/09/measuring-and-magnifying-impact&ved=2ahUKEwjIq5WSi8CAAxVbiVwKHRFRCxcQFnoECCUQAQ&usg=AOvVaw0rJs5u2xRxQ7oE5wCXs9XM

Mullinix B., (Retrieved September 2023)

Startup Cash Flow Management: Unlocking the Secrets

https://www.google.com/url?sa=t&source=web&rct=j&opi=89978449&url=https://www.zeni.ai/blog/startup-cash-flow-management&ved=2ahUKEwi6ppjliMCAAxW8XEEAHat2AlEQFnoECBkQBQ&usg=AOvVaw12EjByDxYdlIcEA9b9Wtly

National Career Service (Retrieved September (2023)

Developing Your Soft Skills

References

https://www.google.com/url?sa=t&source=web&rct=j&opi=89978449&url=https://nationalcareers.service.gov.uk/careers-advice/how-to-develop-your-soft-skills&ved=2ahUKEwiB0bPV-7-AAxWZiFwKHX6kBTkQFnoECCgQAQ&usg=AOvVaw2myYUfo7Av-aifmH1SfVu8

Nanou, E (2022)

How to Make Your Own Career Roadmap (With Templates)

https://www.google.com/url?sa=t&source=web&rct=j&opi=89978449&url=https://www.makeuseof.com/make-career-roadmap-with-templates/&ved=2ahUKEwiP3-TG-L-AAxVRQEEAHWeQAX0QFnoECBQQBQ&usg=AOvVaw38DtU9oO78Bv64Fl37Rvip

National Social Marketing Center (Retrieved September 2023)

Assessing Resources and Risks

https://www.google.com/url?sa=t&source=web&rct=j&opi=89978449&url=https://www.thensmc.com/content/assessing-resources-and-risks-1&ved=2ahUKEwj3zeeXicCAAxX_U0EAHblZDpsQFnoECBIQAQ&usg=AOvVaw18p_8Vpf2GAnaAlQvzW5f6

Neck, H. (2012)

It's Not Failure. It's Intentional Iteration

https://www.google.com/url?sa=t&source=web&rct=j&opi=89978449&url=https://entrepreneurship.babson.edu/its-not-failure-its-intentional-iteration/&ved=2ahUKEwjCo9aJicCAAxWcQUEAHc7PAB4QFnoECCUQAQ&usg=AOvVaw2G8GT9yY9u7x0pUHEb-7xD

Neck, H. (2013)

Entrepreneurs Reframe Failure as Intentional Iteration

https://www.google.com/url?sa=t&source=web&rct=j&opi=89978449&url=https://www.forbes.com/sites/babson/2013/01/28/entrepreneurs-reframe-failure-as-intentional-iteration/amp/&ved=2ahUKEwjCo9aJicCAAxWcQUEAHc7PAB4QFnoECBQQBQ&usg=AOvVaw3WW9XPr5IDluAQd0bR_mpy

Needle, F (2020)

8 Ways Marketers Can Leverage Social Media to Meet Business Objectives

https://www.google.com/url?sa=t&source=web&rct=j&opi=89978449&url=https://blog.hubspot.com/blog/tabid/6307/bid/30888/8-ways-to-leverage-social-media-beyond-social-

networks.aspx&ved=2ahUKEwjSqLuog8CAAxVDh1wKHavNAGAQFnoECDEQAQ&
usg=AOvVaw042Yk-4LfSfMz54ElViPup

Nicastro, S. and Murphy, R (Retrieved September 2023)

How to Write a Business Plan, Step by Step

https://www.google.com/url?sa=t&source=web&rct=j&opi=89978449&url=https://w
ww.nerdwallet.com/article/small-business/business-plan&ved=2ahUKEwii78W-
iMCAAxVLiVwKHT6HC-
8QFnoECA4QBQ&usg=AOvVaw1WbpEcqPgrcDHh5PdWgMRo

Northwestern Pritzker School of Law (2022)

5 Common Legal Issues for Entrepreneurs

https://www.google.com/url?sa=t&source=web&rct=j&opi=89978449&url=https://si
tes.northwestern.edu/mslprogram/2022/07/27/5-common-legal-issues-for-
entrepreneurs/&ved=2ahUKEwiAiOL6iMCAAxVXUkEAHRAwDdkQFnoECA0QAQ&
usg=AOvVaw1WPs2om-kcZRkbBMI5L2cC

Odjick Desirea (2023)

How to Write a Business Plan in 9 Steps

https://www.google.com/url?sa=t&source=web&rct=j&opi=89978449&url=https://w
ww.shopify.com/ng/blog/business-plan&ved=2ahUKEwii78W-
iMCAAxVLiVwKHT6HC-
8QFnoECCgQAQ&usg=AOvVaw3201MgrNoBAZ1M0LxM03kj

OfficeChai (2023)

Exploring Non-Traditional Career Paths

https://www.google.com/url?sa=t&source=web&rct=j&opi=89978449&url=https://o
fficechai.com/miscellaneous/exploring-non-traditional-career-
paths/&ved=2ahUKEwi_prbk97-
AAxW3RUEAHTNjCygQFnoECBcQAQ&usg=AOvVaw1bMeX4Vt5pgAXK9wEB3i8m

Oluwaga, A. (2023)

5 Essential Skills for Thriving in the Digital Age: Unlocking Success in the Modern
Workplace

https://www.google.com/url?sa=t&source=web&rct=j&opi=89978449&url=https://w
ww.linkedin.com/pulse/5-essential-skills-thriving-digital-age-unlocking-success-
oluwaga&ved=2ahUKEwjnoIP-_L-
AAxUNW0EAHQIgCnEQjjh6BAgPEAE&usg=AOvVaw3o5_6CeFUDZnoJ5ek4Gsee

Pappas, C (2023)

References

How to Successfully Navigate Job Interview Obstacles

https://www.google.com/url?sa=t&source=web&rct=j&opi=89978449&url=https://el earningindustry.com/how-to-successfully-navigate-job-interview-obstacles/amp&ved=2ahUKEwiZ_t3egsCAAxUkXEEAHaNcADcQFnoECC0QAQ&usg=AOvVaw25CdsQrZ_KtsYRMB435Svl

Palmer, C (2021)

How to Overcome Imposter Phenomenon

https://www.google.com/url?sa=t&source=web&rct=j&opi=89978449&url=https://www.apa.org/monitor/2021/06/cover-impostor-phenomenon%23:~:text%3DCultivate%2520self%252Dcompassion%26text%3D%25E2%2580%259CWhereas%2520impostor%2520phenomenon%2520is%2520unconscious,are%252C%2520without%2520your%2520accomplishments.%25E2%2580%259D&ved=2ahUKEwiZiurFicCAAxUFR8AKHXBDCV0QFnoECBYQBQ&usg=AOvVaw1pYFSCqIC94WeGKfeY1RQb

Pelta, R (Retrieved September 2023)

15 Transferable Skills That Companies Want: Examples and Definitions

https://www.google.com/url?sa=t&source=web&rct=j&opi=89978449&url=https://www.flexjobs.com/blog/post/transferable-skills/&ved=2ahUKEwiDwdai_L-AAxW8UUEAHcxPC8oQFnoECCsQAQ&usg=AOvVaw14bYWNHjQ1UmotlmJFQdrT

Peterson, T (2023)

Breaking Free from Society's Expectations and Finding Your Tribe

https://www.google.com/url?sa=t&source=web&rct=j&opi=89978449&url=https://www.linkedin.com/pulse/breaking-free-from-societys-expectations-finding-your-karen-petersen&ved=2ahUKEwj2mZK99r-AAxVdW0EAHec5DzYQjjh6BAgTEAE&usg=AOvVaw2HwGu6E8G2DRYYgAVRlf4c

Prpic, N.(2023)

16 Best Online Collaborative Tools (Pros, Cons, Costs, and Ease of Implementation)

https://www.google.com/url?sa=t&source=web&rct=j&opi=89978449&url=https://filestage.io/blog/online-collaboration-tools/&ved=2ahUKEwjWr9mdh8CAAxXaW0EAHRAQA-YQFnoECCUQAQ&usg=AOvVaw0SFyS5L2Ucgk_64QSkyW5C

Rajah, A. (2022)

How to Set Up a Winning Lifestyle for the Long Term

https://www.google.com/url?sa=t&source=web&rct=j&opi=89978449&url=https://www.entrepreneur.com/en-ae/lifestyle/reframing-success-how-to-set-up-a-winning-lifestyle-for/431473&ved=2ahUKEwidqd-ZisCAAxU6QEEAHUIfB2YQFnoECA8QAQ&usg=AOvVaw3Xlmtbuo4-JZ9FjjNBNBjW

Ramsey, P (2023)

Leveraging AI and Open-Source

https://www.google.com/url?sa=t&source=web&rct=j&opi=89978449&url=https://crowdfavorite.com/leveraging-ai-and-open-source/&ved=2ahUKEwio1f_o_L-AAxV3UUEAHYiRBlgQFnoECA8QAQ&usg=AOvVaw37kFy8PoW2-ejyf2t_ujms

Ramsey Solutions (2023)

How to Stick to a Budget

https://www.google.com/url?sa=t&source=web&rct=j&opi=89978449&url=https://www.ramseysolutions.com/budgeting/steps-to-help-you-stick-to-your-budget&ved=2ahUKEwjjhKzAg8CAAxXCnFwKHYwGBEoQFnoECCEQAQ&usg=AOvVaw2-MIPPwV4jojPl2FILvR-Q

Rapacon, S (2023)

Tips for Long-Term Investing

https://www.google.com/url?sa=t&source=web&rct=j&opi=89978449&url=https://www.forbes.com/advisor/investing/tips-for-long-term-investing/&ved=2ahUKEwiP5MHwg8CAAxV6S0EAHRJpBlcQFnoECC0QAQ&usg=AOvVaw1FT3uiVbYHxA8io9eMURpp

Rich, R.S., and Gumpert, E.D (1985)

How to Write a Business Plan

https://www.google.com/url?sa=t&source=web&rct=j&opi=89978449&url=https://hbr.org/1985/05/how-to-write-a-winning-business-plan&ved=2ahUKEwii78W-iMCAAxVLiVwKHT6HC-8QFnoECCIQAQ&usg=AOvVaw0ZlhMfoS6FdzWUwfh6RN3q

Richter, F. (2019)

Leveraging Technology for Social Impact: The Winds of Change are Here

https://www.google.com/url?sa=t&source=web&rct=j&opi=89978449&url=https://horasis.org/leveraging-technology-for-social-impact-the-winds-of-change-are-here/&ved=2ahUKEwiHjfDOisCAAxXXgVwKHQPyA0cQFnoECA0QAQ&usg=AOvVaw1KaWsh1GjcqA-qlz_ptNuT

References

RocheMartin (2022)

50 Tips for Improving Your Emotional Intelligence

https://www.google.com/url?sa=t&source=web&rct=j&opi=89978449&url=https://www.rochemartin.com/blog/50-tips-improving-emotional-intelligence&ved=2ahUKEwi6wJy5icCAAxXnXUEAHWkuCTUQFnoECBAQBQ&usg=AOvVaw1Tk-9mKYtyiXX22R2yKd5E

Samjudin, M.R.B (2023)

The Art of Job Hunting

https://www.google.com/url?sa=t&source=web&rct=j&opi=89978449&url=https://www.linkedin.com/pulse/art-job-hunting-mohd-rizal-bin-samjudin-hcip&ved=2ahUKEwjm6sv1gcCAAxV-XUEAHTEqAyQQjjh6BAgjEAE&usg=AOvVaw04AP8HBqFozNXecpTUTaol

Sean, P (2023)

Work-Life Balance: How to Set Manageable Boundaries

https://www.google.com/url?sa=t&source=web&rct=j&opi=89978449&url=https://www.business.com/articles/work-life-boundaries/&ved=2ahUKEwjd9_Wzh8CAAxWHLcAKHVyvARMQFnoECCsQAQ&usg=AOvVaw0RsCoG9ncLPQx4TWlwhXY9

SecurianFinancial (Retrieved September 2023)

5 Steps to Building an Emergency Fund

https://www.google.com/url?sa=t&source=web&rct=j&opi=89978449&url=https://www.securian.com/insights-tools/articles/5-steps-to-building-an-emergency-fund.html&ved=2ahUKEwj4uqalhMCAAxUtWEEAHRvrBOwQFnoECBEQAQ&usg=AOvVaw0jF3x3zSneA26m71bnBwd7

Segal, J. et al (2023)

Improving Emotional Intelligence

https://www.google.com/url?sa=t&source=web&rct=j&opi=89978449&url=https://www.helpguide.org/articles/mental-health/emotional-intelligence-eq.htm&ved=2ahUKEwi6wJy5icCAAxXnXUEAHWkuCTUQFnoECDwQAQ&usg=AOvVaw0TUXGeD7T7yOVMQEOJniwB

Slack Team (2021)

10 Tips for Effective Time Management at Work

https://www.google.com/url?sa=t&source=web&rct=j&opi=89978449&url=https://slack.com/blog/collaboration/mastering-time-management-at-

work&ved=2ahUKEwjs0MT-
hsCAAxVCh1wKHf3yBScQFnoECBEQAQ&usg=AOvVaw2UK0if5eO9VkEVHR_-
38Lb

Sparkpress (Retrieved September 2023)

6 Tips for Handling Rejection and Taking Criticism

https://www.google.com/url?sa=t&source=web&rct=j&opi=89978449&url=https://g
osparkpress.com/6-tips-for-handling-rejection-and-taking-
criticism/&ved=2ahUKEwjL2KPSicCAAxXjQkEAHT9fA00QFnoECEkQAQ&usg=AOv
Vaw2K8aKulHDMBekFTY9Qkz20

Stiles, C. (2023)

Embracing Lifelong Learning: A Journey of Growth and Discovery

https://www.google.com/url?sa=t&source=web&rct=j&opi=89978449&url=https://w
ww.linkedin.com/pulse/embracing-lifelong-learning-journey-growth-discovery-
chris-stiles&ved=2ahUKEwiw1u3j_b-
AAxV5WEEAHWWjAisQjjh6BAgdEAE&usg=AOvVaw3-rqSxDfanhfGqnYQ8eF22

Strathmore University Business School (2023)

Top 10 Technology-Driven Jobs of the Future

https://www.google.com/url?sa=t&source=web&rct=j&opi=89978449&url=https://s
bs.strathmore.edu/top-10-technology-driven-jobs-of-the-
future/&ved=2ahUKEwjl76i8hsCAAxXLYcAKHVdBBqsQFnoECCwQAQ&usg=AOvV
aw3dJnvHYnlwZoK8caNv8Htu

Sullivan, R. (2022)

The Do's and Don'ts of Effective Virtual Communication

https://www.google.com/url?sa=t&source=web&rct=j&opi=89978449&url=https://w
ww.hartfordfunds.com/practice-management/practice-management-
strategies/communicate-to-connect/the-dos-and-donts-of-effective-virtual-
communication.html&ved=2ahUKEwiAwfiNh8CAAxULR8AKHc2PDHkQFnoECBIQ
AQ&usg=AOvVaw2GP4w6RVygzgjBUxd5iFne

The Jinn Team (2023)

Exploring Non-Traditional Career Paths: Opportunities Outside the Norm

https://www.google.com/url?sa=t&source=web&rct=j&opi=89978449&url=https://ji
nn.careers/blog/career/non-traditional-
careers/%23:~:text%3DMany%2520people%2520are%2520curious%2520about,
%252C%2520remote%2520work%252C%2520and%2520more.&ved=2ahUKEwi

prbk97-
AAxW3RUEAHTNjCygQFnoECBIQBQ&usg=AOvVaw0kGwl3DBTZVtxgO8hB-CQk

The University of Texas Permian Basin(Retrieved September 2023)

Balancing Long-Term and Short-Term Financial Planning

https://www.google.com/url?sa=t&source=web&rct=j&opi=89978449&url=https://o
nline.utpb.edu/about-us/articles/business/balancing-long-term-and-short-term-
financial-
planning&ved=2ahUKEwjki8jWhMCAAxXOTEEAHZYkDXgQFnoECCYQAQ&usg=A
OvVaw1-sOSwA8MRmADuxxU7A83G

Thompson, S. (2017)

5 Ways to Use Online Collaboration Tools for eLearning Projects

https://www.google.com/url?sa=t&source=web&rct=j&opi=89978449&url=https://el
earningindustry.com/online-collaboration-tools-for-elearning-projects-5-
ways/amp&ved=2ahUKEwjWr9mdh8CAAxXaW0EAHRAQA-
YQFnoECBAQAQ&usg=AOvVaw1OM9sy52VM8r1QWyWIxjJX

Tomaszewski, M (2023)

How to Make a Resume That Stands Out: Examples and Tips

https://www.google.com/url?sa=t&source=web&rct=j&opi=89978449&url=https://z
ety.com/blog/make-your-resume-stand-
out&ved=2ahUKEwi7vvjTgcCAAxVRQEEAHWeQAX0QFnoECCoQAQ&usg=AOvVa
w2KnSSuz6z9nqky-DyUOoPD

Tracy, B (Retrieved September 2023)

7 Time Management Tips to Help You Master Productivity

https://www.google.com/url?sa=t&source=web&rct=j&opi=89978449&url=https://w
ww.briantracy.com/blog/time-management/time-management-
tips/&ved=2ahUKEwjs0MT-
hsCAAxVCh1wKHf3yBScQFnoECC8QAQ&usg=AOvVaw1OIwwV2SkwfesfLHHhUV
sC

University of Hawaii at Manoa Library (2023)

Industry Information

https://www.google.com/url?sa=t&source=web&rct=j&opi=89978449&url=https://g
uides.library.manoa.hawaii.edu/c.php%3Fg%3D105699%26p%3D687820%23:~:t
ext%3DGather%2520information%2520to%2520determine%2520the,for%2520la
rge%2520and%2520small%2520industries.&ved=2ahUKEwi6rrbeh8CAAxWXi1w
KHVjZCeQQFnoECBEQBQ&usg=AOvVaw0RcCgSNoi2g47xlsHgC93G

Urban, E (2018)

How to Focus Your Unique Strengths to Maximize Your Potential

https://www.google.com/url?sa=t&source=web&rct=j&opi=89978449&url=https://www.linkedin.com/pulse/how-find-focus-your-unique-strengths-maximize-erin-urban-lssbb-cpdc&ved=2ahUKEwizwl6t9r-AAxUFBMAKHSUECzsQjjh6BAhLEAE&usg=AOvVaw29U8AEirXitO8yOdlX9Ng4

Vaughin, C (2022)

The 9 Best Tips for Showcasing Your Portfolio to Employers

https://www.google.com/url?sa=t&source=web&rct=j&opi=89978449&url=https://www.makeuseof.com/best-tips-for-showcasing-portfolio-to-employers/&ved=2ahUKEwiE7vrD_r

Whatman, P (2021)

A Deep Dive into Startup Cash Flow Management

https://www.google.com/url?sa=t&source=web&rct=j&opi=89978449&url=https://www.spendesk.com/en-eu/blog/startup-cash-flow-management/&ved=2ahUKEwi6ppjliMCAAxW8XEEAHat2AIEQFnoECBoQAQ&usg=AOvVaw2ZONk9MJz_SeEw5X4zazN-

WEF (2022)

Should You Go Freelance? Here's What You Need to Know about the Gig Economy

https://www.google.com/url?sa=t&source=web&rct=j&opi=89978449&url=https://www.weforum.org/agenda/2022/09/freelance-gig-economy-work/&ved=2ahUKEwib1e2Fq8CAAxW1RkEAHeBpD80QFnoECBEQAQ&usg=AOvVaw3_2dhERmNNMr5AdPjKW9Qa

Warner, M. M. (2020)

How to Break Free from Society's Expectations

https://www.google.com/url?sa=t&source=web&rct=j&opi=89978449&url=https://medium.com/the-partnered-pen/how-to-break-free-from-societys-expectations-4293faa28202&ved=2ahUKEwj2mZK99r-AAxVdWOEAHec5DzYQFnoECC4QAQ&usg=AOvVaw3MZjTGuuaExxt5MtVKKYuJ

Wooll, M. (2022)

How to Find Your Passion and Discover Your Zest for Life (2022)

https://www.google.com/url?sa=t&source=web&rct=j&opi=89978449&url=https://www.betterup.com/blog/how-to-find-your-passion%3Fhs_amp%3Dtrue&ved=2ahUKEwj8_vGd9r-

References

AAxWzRkEAHc3kAmQQFnoECAwQAQ&usg=AOvVaw3YwKps3g8t1WNXEWvPRB
kC

Wooll, M (2022)

How to Increase Adaptability in an Ever-Changing World

https://www.google.com/url?sa=t&source=web&rct=j&opi=89978449&url=https://w
ww.betterup.com/blog/how-to-increase-
adaptability%3Fhs_amp%3Dtrue&ved=2ahUKEwinj7L-
hMCAAxXFV0EAHSVHDsYQFnoECCIQAQ&usg=AOvVaw06WWD8sDcEWT99clZr
WsqP

YoungPeopleToday (2022)

How Young People Can Position Their Brand for Success

https://www.google.com/url?sa=t&source=web&rct=j&opi=89978449&url=https://w
ww.youngpeopletoday.net/young-entrepreneurs-positioning-successful-
brand/&ved=2ahUKEwj1vLXQiMCAAxWPSUEAHVnpD70QFnoECC0QAQ&usg=AO
vVaw29UMoBu76kl5w2Ip2CjE_e

Other References

https://www.google.com/url?sa=t&source=web&rct=j&opi=89978449&url=https://w
ww.wrike.com/remote-work-guide/faq/what-is-remote-work-
revolution/&ved=2ahUKEwiKx4bnhsCAAxUpQEEAHaROBQ4QFnoECF8QAQ&usg=
AOvVaw0oaZbJzMxOAVEzCIGXXiZw (Retrieved September 2023)

https://www.google.com/url?sa=t&source=web&rct=j&opi=89978449&url=https://w
ww.entrepreneur.com/growing-a-business/the-entrepreneurs-comprehensive-
guide-to-navigating-
legal/450166&ved=2ahUKEwiAiOL6iMCAAxVXUkEAHRAwDdkQFnoECBAQAQ&us
g=AOvVaw0WzzLPBCT3OH9CZ83wa_pc (Retrieved September 2023)

https://www.google.com/url?sa=t&source=web&rct=j&opi=89978449&url=https://w
ww.waldenu.edu/why-walden/social-change/resource/four-small-ways-to-make-
a-big-social-change-impact&ved=2ahUKEwior-
b3isCAAxWOVUEAHYVDAisQFnoECCoQAQ&usg=AOvVaw3zwEaJ0QoBnABxLy7k
PTmD (Retrieved September 2023)

https://www.google.com/url?sa=t&source=web&rct=j&opi=89978449&url=https://b
usinesscollective.com/7-ways-to-build-the-ultimate-support-
network/index.html&ved=2ahUKEwizx7bhicCAAxVJFcAKHY27BaUQFnoECBEQAQ
&usg=AOvVaw1z10daKN8ie8r3_tb1flMb (Retrieved September 2023)

https://www.google.com/url?sa=t&source=web&rct=j&opi=89978449&url=https://u
praise.io/blog/10-effective-communication-tips-for-virtual-
teams/&ved=2ahUKEwiAwfiNh8CAAxULR8AKHc2PDHkQFnoECCMQAQ&usg=AO
vVaw0qeL3VZk6ZmWPwCx-fy-Dp (Retrieved September 2023)

https://www.google.com/url?sa=t&source=web&rct=j&opi=89978449&url=https://w
ww.uopeople.edu/blog/10-successful-entrepreneurs-started-with-
nothing/&ved=2ahUKEwjPlrHx97-AAxXWTkEAHZ--
D68QFnoECCAQAQ&usg=AOvVaw0ODzzUkc_yWgtZd9rQxKQo   (Retrieved
September 2023)

https://www.google.com/url?sa=t&source=web&rct=j&opi=89978449&url=https://w
ww.briantracy.com/blog/personal-success/goal-setting/&ved=2ahUKEwio8Lue-L-
AAxW2XEEAHZsbBT0QFnoECD8QAQ&usg=AOvVaw3Tj4AXKMFuGlwKtEEKtnJW
(Retrieved September 2023)

https://www.google.com/url?sa=t&source=web&rct=j&opi=89978449&url=https://w
ww.lucidchart.com/blog/time-management-at-work&ved=2ahUKEwjsOMT-
hsCAAxVCh1wKHf3yBScQFnoECBIQBQ&usg=AOvVaw0Fee-ot0tk4Qu7tRc2mhZY
(Retrieved September 2023)

https://www.google.com/url?sa=t&source=web&rct=j&opi=89978449&url=https://w
ww.mapfre.com.mt/blog/nurturing-resilience-building-mental-strength-and-
adaptability/%23:~:text%3DBy%2520cultivating%2520a%2520growth%2520mind
set,challenges%2520with%2520strength%2520and%2520adaptability.&ved=2ah
UKEwiSpfWqicCAAxV6S0EAHRJpBlcQFnoECA8QBQ&usg=AOvVaw3vYbbifjACwB
r7fL3XlwTZ (Retrieved September 2023)

https://www.google.com/url?sa=t&source=web&rct=j&opi=89978449&url=https://v
arthana.com/student/how-to-navigate-your-way-through-job-interview-
rounds/%23:~:text%3DNavigating%2520through%2520job%2520interview%2520
rounds,ask%2520questions%252C%2520and%2520follow%2520up.&ved=2ahUK
EwiZ_t3egsCAAxUkXEEAHaNcADcQFnoECAwQBQ&usg=AOvVaw1UGE4Btw4NM
QpQml7zQjTm (Retrieved September 2023)

https://www.google.com/url?sa=t&source=web&rct=j&opi=89978449&url=https://w
ww.valamis.com/hub/lifelong-learning&ved=2ahUKEwiw1u3j_b-
AAxV5WEEAHWWjAisQFnoECDkQAQ&usg=AOvVaw1_VzsPr1GEHx0i1KlwAWVK
(Retrieved September 2023)

https://www.google.com/url?sa=t&source=web&rct=j&opi=89978449&url=https://w
ww.netacad.com/careers/career-advice/how-to-gain-experience/advice-finding-
and-leveraging-mentorship&ved=2ahUKEwjL5Ni--b-
AAxXxW0EAHXDzDO0QFnoECBQQAQ&usg=AOvVaw1WL5gOpRrYCSvym3pajYb
L (Retrieved September 2023)

References

https://www.google.com/url?sa=t&source=web&rct=j&opi=89978449&url=https://marketinsights.citi.com/Financial-Guidance/Investing/Steps-to-Building-Your-Portfolio.html&ved=2ahUKEwinhLnugsCAAxXKEsAKHbHbC8AQFnoECBQQBQ&usg=AOvVaw3yPtJoQjNw2ECe8vQh2Dhc (Retrieved September 2023)

https://www.google.com/url?sa=t&source=web&rct=j&opi=89978449&url=https://www.debt.org/credit/%23:~:text%3DCredit%2520vs.,owe%2520at%2520any%2520given%2520time.&ved=2ahUKEwjYq9Lhg8CAAxVdQUEAHd8hDHUQFnoECAwQBQ&usg=AOvVaw0E_2bPgIgUff4Wx_DScLKu (Retrieved September 2023)

https://www.google.com/url?sa=t&source=web&rct=j&opi=89978449&url=https://in.indeed.com/career-advice/career-development/how-to-make-portfolio&ved=2ahUKEwinhLnugsCAAxXKEsAKHbHbC8AQFnoECBoQAQ&usg=AOvVaw2TpddAm-vrE48ISDiWBgOW (Retrieved September 2023)

https://www.google.com/url?sa=t&source=web&rct=j&opi=89978449&url=https://students.1fbusa.com/pay-it-forward/25-ways-to-volunteer-in-your-community&ved=2ahUKEwjijP3eisCAAxXZRkEAHZyBBGcQFnoECCYQAQ&usg=AOvVaw0bG2-646hX-pt-259SJpFC (Retrieved September 2023)

https://www.google.com/url?sa=t&source=web&rct=j&opi=89978449&url=https://www.123financials.com/insights/startup-cash-flow-management/&ved=2ahUKEwi6ppjliMCAAxW8XEEAHat2AIEQFnoECCUQAQ&usg=AOvVaw2ObLgox-ptLTgp3EzO-3xo (Retrieved September 2023)

www.ingramcontent.com/pod-product-compliance
Lightning Source LLC
Chambersburg PA
CBHW060447280326
41933CB00014B/2695